A Collection of Recipes from

Cucina Lucia

Sicilian Cooking & Baking

with

Maria Indelicato

Printed in the U.S.A. by

P.O. Box 2110 • Kearney, NE 68848
800-445-6621 • www.morriscookbooks.com

My dear readers,

I hope you will enjoy this book as much as I enjoyed bringing it to life! It took me almost two years to cook, bake, and create all of our family recipes which were never written down. I wrote these recipes the way my mother explained things to me as we cooked and baked together through the years. It is how I learned to make all of her "recipes." As you read our recipes, you might feel as if my mother is standing next to you, explaining how to do things the same way she did for me.

In the process of creating this cookbook, I discovered that I have memories that go with each recipe. I wanted to share these memories with you. The stories are what make this book more than a cookbook. They are what make it special!

I hope you will enjoy my stories and cooking and baking our special dishes from Pozzallo and Siculiana, Sicily.

Sincerely,

Maria Indelicato

Meet Maria...

I was born on January 25, 1954 in Auburn, NY, and it is where I grew up.

I have two children, Pam and Tommy. Being their mother is the best and most rewarding part of my life. I have two step-daughters, Libby and Chelsey, and three grandchildren.

In 2010, I moved to Fort Myers, Florida, three miles from the Causeway to Sanibel Island. Blind Pass Beach, on Sanibel, is my favorite place in the world. I am an avid sea shell collector and use them to make treasures which I sell. Sanibel is my peaceful place where I am happiest!

I have four wonderful children, beautiful grandchildren, I live by the beach where there are sea shells, sand, the Gulf of Mexico, and where the sun shines 271 days a year. There is nothing more I could want in this life! I'm living my dream!

Pam & Tommy 2016

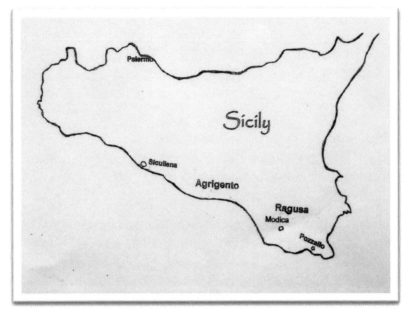

Where We Are From...

Mom's family is from Pozzallo & Modica in Sicily.

Dad's family is from Siculiana, Sicily.

All of our family recipes are from these small coastal towns.

Special Times...

Mom & Dad's wedding,
November 3, 1945
Nona & Nono Ruta on left,
Nona & Nono Indelicato
on right.

Mom & Me

Mom Lucia's 85th
Birthday!

Meet Lucia...

I wrote this book in honor of my mother, Lucy Ruta Indelicato.
She was an amazing lady and a loving mother and
grandmother. Everyone loved her. These are her recipes.
Without her, this book wouldn't be possible. Now, her recipes
will live on as long as people keep cooking and baking them. It
is my honor to be her daughter!

Welcome to Cucina Lucia

In our Sicilian dialect, Cucina means kitchen. Lucia was my mother. Starting when I was a little girl, I spent endless hours with my mother in her kitchen, Cucina Lucia, learning how to cook and bake our family's Sicilian foods and making memories that would last a lifetime. She was a fabulous cook. My mother's "recipes" were passed down through generations but most were never written down.

When I spoke to people whose roots are Sicilian or Italian, I discovered that recipes with the same name are very different. They vary from city to city. When I mention our "Sicilian Baked Macaroni," people think it is the same as baked ziti. It isn't. When I mention "Sweet Ravioli," people tell me that there is no such thing. There is. As you look over my family's recipes in Cucina Lucia, Sicilian Cooking & Baking, you will discover the many dishes that came from the small cities in Sicily from which my family came. The photos of our foods will make you hungry!

Most of the recipes in this book are my maternal grandmother's, my Nona Ruta's recipes that originated in Pozzallo, Sicily, the town from which my mother's family came to America. Recipes passed down on my father's side of the family originated in Siculiana, Sicily. Pozzallo is located in the province of Ragusa and Siculiana is located in the province of Agrigento.

To enjoy our authentic and unique Sicilian "recipes," you can make them yourself, go to Sicily, or, if you are lucky, you have a Sicilian friend that loves to cook and bake!

I

Creating Family Recipes

Creating my family's Sicilian recipes was important to me so that I could pass them down to the next generation. I didn't want our unique recipes to die with me. It was a goal that took much time, thought, research and learning. I spent endless hours in the kitchen building my recipes, with ingredient lists and directions, for the sixty plus recipes included in this book. For over a year, I cooked, baked, measured, tasted, took notes, wrote things down, altered measurements, and then started all over again until I got it right. I also managed to gain thirty pounds; but it was worth every delicious bite!

Memories that came back to me while I was doing all of these things were an unexpected surprise. I realized that each of my recipes had a story behind it and decided to include these in my book. Most of the stories in this book are as I remember them while others are stories that people told me through the years. My mother used to tell me the stories about her family and her experiences during her lifetime. Those of you who have been in my life probably remember things differently. I hope you enjoy my renditions.

Sharing my family's recipes with people who love to cook and bake, who want to try something new and exciting, and that have a desire to learn about Sicilian cooking and baking was something else I wanted to do. I invite you to try my family's authentic Sicilian recipes and find out for yourself how unique and delicious they truly are!

"Cucina Povera"

"Cucina Povera," in Sicilian, means poor kitchen, but the dishes my mother, her mother before her, and now I prepare, are anything but "poor." They are simple and budget friendly recipes that feed a large family and are a culinary experience!

Growing up on a farm during the Great Depression, money was scarce for my grandparents and their children. They lived on a farm and had a large garden to grow what they needed to feed their family. They canned fruits and vegetables for the winter. At the grocery stores, food was rationed and there were limits on how much they could purchase of certain items. When they shopped for food, they had to have their ration books with them.

My mother, Lucia, recounted a story about she and her father driving in a blizzard on the country road leading to their house. The drifts of snow caused their car to slide into a ditch. They walked to a neighboring farm in the blowing snow and frigid temperature for help. Upon their arrival they realized that their family's ration books had been left in the car. My mother walked back to the car in the cold blowing snow and deep drifts to get them. Without them, they would not be allowed to buy food.

I was always amazed at how far my mother could stretch a dollar. We were a family of five. We ate pasta dishes four times a week but always had steak, mashed potatoes, and a vegetable on Saturday. Being Catholic, we ate fish on Friday. We always had salads with my mother's dressing of olive oil, vinegar, salt, and pepper in just the right proportions without using a "recipe."

With a cup of flour, a little salt, eggs, and home-made sauce, I can make an incredibly delicious dinner of home-made pasta. With another cup of flour, eggs, sugar and milk, I can make a special dessert fit for the holidays, one being Cream Puffs with Sicilian Cream.

I invite you to try some of our unique Sicilian recipes from the small towns of Pozzallo and Siculiana in Sicily. My family brought these recipes with them to America and you will see that you can feed your family well on a budget.

"We had a fig tree growing behind our garage. Each year it produced about five figs. Fig trees didn't grow in our climate, so before winter my mother dug a trench, loosened the soil around the roots of the tree, laid it down in the trench, and buried it until the next summer!"

Coming To America

In 1920 my maternal grandfather, Rosario, came to America to make a better life for his family. He was born in Pozzalo, Sicily, in the Province of Ragusa, and when he married my grandmother, Maria, they lived in Modica, also located in Ragusa, where my mother, Lucia, was born. When he left Sicily, my grandmother was pregnant for their first child, my mother. For almost seven years, my grandfather was only able to see his wife and young daughter in photographs.

V

In 1927, he was finally able to send for them and bring them to America. My mother, Lucia, was six years old and my grandmother, Maria, was twenty-seven. At the port in Palermo, they hugged and kissed their family good-bye, knowing they would never see them again.

I envision my grandmother holding the hand of her young daughter as they walked up the ramp to board the Martha Washington, bringing with them all of their worldly possessions. The Martha Washington left Palermo on August 12, 1927. They traveled "Biglietto di Seconda Classe Economica," which was Second Class Economy, and were assigned to Cabin #233. They arrived at Ellis Island on August 27, 1927. They came to America for a better life but left behind so much that was dear to them.

The trip was not without turmoil. On August 24, a hurricane struck that reached the Atlantic Ocean. It was reported to be the worst storm in many years. As the ship rocked, pushed on its side by the gigantic waves that hit it, people held on to tables and chairs, crying and screaming from fear, and praying to reach the harbor. The only memory my mother had of the trip was that people were sea sick. My mother's sister, Margaret, told me that her mother, my grandmother, laughed. She thought it was funny that people were getting sick. But they were sick and scared for good reason. I have wondered if my grandmother laughed so that my mother wouldn't be scared. The passengers, and crew alike, were relieved when they reached the port at Ellis Island.

Life in America proved to be different from life in Sicily. In Sicily, everyone drank wine, even the children, because the drinking water was not safe.

My mother told me a story about a time, soon after arriving in America, that she drank too much wine and her father found her in a ditch by the road! He just thought she was "his little drunk!" She was only six years old!

More children started coming, all born at home on the farm. My grandfather's brother's wife, Angie, was the midwife who delivered all six of my grandmother's babies. My mother told me that when she was growing up, she didn't have any dolls. Her "dolls" were her baby brothers and sisters that she dressed, took care of, and with whom she played.

My grandfather had two brothers who had also come to America and lived on the same street in Auburn, NY, but my grandfather lived on a farm four miles out of the city. When my grandparents got older, they wanted to move to the city. My grandfather was afraid that in an emergency, in the winter, no one would be able to get to them. They moved into a house on the same street as his brothers.

In March of 1974, my grandmother woke up to find that my grandfather had died in his sleep. She called my mother who had to call the city for a snowplow so an emergency vehicle could get to their house. It was during a March snow storm that brought five feet of snow! The irony is that even after moving to the city, what my grandfather feared the most had happened.

The night before my grandfather passed away, I was working three quarters of a mile from home. The snowstorm kept me from getting home. Even in March we had snowstorms that paralyzed our city.

Waiting In Sicily

In 1888, in Siculiana, Sicily, my grandfather, Vincenzo, was born. The first time he came to America was in June of 1913 on the ship, Luisiana. He was 25 years old. When he first came to America, he left behind his wife, Mariantonia, and his son, Melchiorre, who was my father. He went back to Sicily in 1916 and 1919 and they had daughters Vincenza and Francesca. He returned to America and worked so he could send money back to his wife, son, and daughters until he was able to bring them to America.

When my grandfather first came to America, he worked in a glass factory, in Kokomo, Indiana, until it closed. With some of his cousins, who had also come to the United States, he traveled to different cities to look for work. When they arrived in Auburn, NY, he and his cousins lived there together and my grandfather opened a butcher shop.

In Siculiana, Sicily, my grandmother, Mariantonia, her sister Mariassunta, and their mother, Francesca, owned a store near the fishing port, Scalo Marina. They were business women who bought sardines and anchovies, off the boats that came in each day, to sell in their store. My father worked on a fishing boat but work was scarce, so when he was 16 years old, he came to America to be with his father and find work. He came on the ship Saturnia in 1929.

My grandfather had become a United States citizen when he lived in Kokomo, Indiana, so when my father was twenty-one, he automatically became a citizen.

In 1938 my grandfather sent for his wife and daughters. Vincenza was married so she remained in Sicily with her husband. My grandmother and aunt, Francesca, came to America on the ship Saturnia from Palermo, Sicily. My aunt was 19 years old at the time. When they arrived in Auburn, jobs were scarce. Eventually Francesca found a job as a seamstress, making pockets for men's vests, in a factory in Auburn, NY. It was hard work, piece-work, and the seamstresses were paid for how many pieces they could make each day. She worked there for 20 years, until it closed, and soon found a job working at Learbury's, in Syracuse, NY, making sleeves for men's suit jackets. She worked there until she retired to care for my grandmother in old age. My grandmother lived to the age of 92. Her sister, my great-aunt, Mariassunta, lived to the age of 98. My aunt, Vincenza, passed away at the age of 94. In 2016, my aunt, Francesca, was 97 and was still living independently.

When my ancestors came to Auburn, NY, they lived among the people who lived with them in the same cities in Sicily and who had also come to America for a better life. They were their "paisans." They had the same customs, ate the same foods, spoke the same Sicilian dialect, lived in neighborhoods together, worshipped at the same church and celebrated special occasions together. Through the years, the bonds remained strong. We would get together with our "paisans" to enjoy food, drink, and lots of laughter. One of the men, bringing his love of music to his new country, played his guitar and sang, keeping their music alive.

I think of how difficult it must have been leaving their families behind, to never see them again, and moving to this new country where everything was different from anything they knew. I think of my father, Melchiorre, and my grandmother, Mariantonia, who after coming to America, never went back to Sicily. They never again saw their family members that they left behind, which included my father's grandmother, my grandmother's mother. After my grandfather sent for his wife and daughter, he also never returned to Sicily.

My aunt, Francesca, went back to Sicily two times after moving to the United States. She went back to attend her niece Pietra's wedding. The second and last time she went back to Sicily was for Pietra's funeral, when sadly, she passed away at the age of 42.

While I was learning about my family and all they endured to come to America to create a better life, emotions came flooding in. I laughed and I cried. I've learned so much about my roots but I know there is still much to discover and more family I have yet to meet. I am looking forward to what the future brings.

Photo on page VIII: Dad Melchiorre, Nona Indelicato, Aunt Francesca

Eight Melchiorres

My paternal grandfather, Vincenzo, was one of eight brothers. It is the custom for a married couple of Sicilian descent to name their firstborn son after his father and their second son after her father.

My grandfather and his seven brothers each named their first son Melchiorre and they all lived in Siculiana. My father, who was one of the eight Melchiorres, told me that when the cousins walked down the street together, they were called by their fathers' names to distinguish between them. So instead of being called Melchiorre, they were called Baldasaro, Gasparo and Melchiorre, brothers who were named after the three wise men, and Vincenzo, Pasquale, Alfonso, Giusseppe, and Carmelo.

Until 2015, I only knew about three Melchiorres; my father, Zizi Mike, from Rochester, NY, and Melchiorre, from Galesburg, IL. My father had three children, Vincent, Rosario, and me, Maria. Zizi Mike, as we called him, never had any children. Melchiorre, from Galesburg, had Alfonso, Joseph, Salvatore, and Patrina. He came to America with his wife, Sarina, and their children in 1954 on the Andrea Doria.

Melchiorre, from Galesburg, had a brother Giuseppe whose children include Alan, Pat, Joanne and Anne Marie. Giuseppe came to America with his mother, Pietra, in 1934. When WWII broke out, he enlisted in the American army. When he was stationed in Melbourne, Australia, he met his future wife, Yvonnette, who later came to America where they were married. I met Pat and her husband, Leonard, when they came to visit me in the summer of 2015. Until I met Pat, I never saw this photograph of my great-grandfather, Melchiorre Indelicato, after whom my father and his seven cousins were named.

In 2015, I was told about another Melchiorre who lived in Sicily his entire life. I do not know his wife's or daughter's name, but their sons were Melchiorre and Antonino.

I discovered that one of my cousins, Joe, and his wife, Sharon, live four miles away from me. It is amazing since the city we live in is a large city. It was a wonderful surprise to find family that live nearby!

With almost all of the older generation of Indelicatos gone, it is difficult to learn more about those who came before us. Going forward may bring some surprises that will certainly be interesting. We still might discover more of us that have the same great-grandfather, and that relationship gives us a connection that will last forever!

Arranged Marriage

In Sicily, arranged marriages were common, but not so much in the United States, even in 1945. Some friends, "paisans," knew both my mother's and father's families and thought that they would be a good match. They arranged for them to meet in hopes of a marriage. My mother was twenty-five and my father was thirty-two. In August of 1945, my father's family visited my mother's family on the farm to introduce them. This was the first time they met.

Shortly after meeting and accepting his marriage proposal, they had an engagement party. On November 3, 1945, they were married at St. Francis of Assisi Church in Auburn, NY with all of their family and friends there to celebrate.

My mother looked beautiful in her white satin wedding gown with a long trailing veil. My father's sister, Francesca, was her maid of honor and her cousins were bridesmaids. My father's best man was my mother's brother, Salvatore.

The following year, my oldest brother, Vincent, was born. My brother, Rosario, was born 4 years later, and I followed three and a half years later. When I was with my mother and she introduced me to someone, she always said, "This is my Mary," even when I was over fifty years old!

My mother and father were married for 42 years when my father, Melchiorre, passed away shortly after being diagnosed with cancer in 1986. He was seventy-two years old. My mother, Lucia, sadly passed away in 2006 at the age of 86. She was an independent and strong lady.

After my mother passed away, I found the mementos she saved throughout her life; the plans for her wedding that she had written down, their wedding guest list, the gifts they received, and their wedding cards. She saved the cards she received when my brothers and I were born, our childhood birthday cards, our school pictures, and every report card.

I also learned that babies come with directions! I discovered little books that told a mother how to care for her new baby. The first book was given to the mother when the baby was born and more little books followed every three months! They instructed the mother when, what, and how much to feed her baby, how many ounces the baby should gain each month, how much the baby should sleep, and what milestones a baby should be reaching at each age. I always used to say that babies should come with directions, and I discovered that they did!

State Street Sporting Goods Store

When we look back at our lives, we have memories that stay with us more than others. I can remember when I was a little girl, sitting on top of a glass display case in my parents' sporting goods store. I was around 5 years old.

My mother told me that my father always wanted his own sporting goods store. The street where our house was located was zoned residential. My parents were required to go to each neighbor, ask them if they would allow the area to be zoned business, and get the required number of signatures so they could go into business. The city approved their business zoning and they opened their store.

With $500.00, my mother and father opened State Street Sporting Goods, in 1954, in the sun porch of our house on State Street, of course! They found vendors and set up their store with glass cases, racks, and shelves and filled them with all the things people needed to fish, hunt or trap. They also sold live bait. Worms were in wooden boxes and minnows and crabs were in the cement tanks my father built in the basement.

When you have your own business, and it is in your house, you are always there and always available. The store opened early in the morning and stayed open until late at night; but there was a bell near the front door. On opening days of fishing, customers would be at our door ringing the bell, to get their live bait, at 4:00 in the morning. This was also the case on the opening day of deer hunting season; men buying ammunition and other last minute supplies. My parents never turned customers away. Their motto was, "Always here to serve you."

Running the store was hard work. In the winter, they ran the store together. In the summer months, my mother ran it alone during the day as my father worked full-time in road construction. He had a very hard job.

The store did well and eventually they needed a bigger space. They had a larger store built and my best friends' father, who built homes and other buildings, built the new store across the front of our house, in place of the porch that had been there. I remember that when I was a little girl, before the store was built, I could climb out of my bedroom window onto the porch. I also remember my family sitting on the front porch, talking with neighbors.

My parents, brothers and I used to go out at night to pick worms to sell in the store; my brothers and parents more than me because I was younger.

The neighborhood kids also picked worms for my father and he paid them a fair price. Years later these grown up "kids" would tell me how they earned money by picking worms for my father. For many, this was a first job.

It really was amazing what my father could do. He made sinkers by melting lead and pouring it into forms. He also repaired everything from fishing poles and reels to Coleman lanterns and stoves.

One Halloween, when I was about 10 years old, after going trick-or-treating, I had more candy than I could ever eat. I asked my parents if we could sell it in the store. It went over big! The wholesaler that supplied cigarettes to our store also sold candy, so candy bars were ordered and we started selling them. Large size candy bars cost 5 cents, and at that time cigarettes cost 28 cents. After school, kids would come to our store to buy candy bars. Every time the door opened, a bell rang in our kitchen and my mother would run to the store to sell candy to the kids. From that time on, we sold candy in our store until the day it closed.

Because we sold candy bars, I was never at a loss for candy. I was allowed to take candy from the store but would never take anything unless I told my parents I was taking something. That's just the way we were raised. Because candy was always available, I am not a real candy lover. I love chocolate but don't eat a lot of candy bars. And those same 5 cent candy bars sell for over a dollar these days!

Because of the way I was raised, and trusted, if I needed money, my mother would tell me to take it out of her wallet.

I would take exactly what I needed and not one penny more. When my kids were growing up, I did the same, telling them to take it out of my wallet. They would take exactly how much they needed. If I wasn't near my purse when the kids needed money, they would take what they needed and leave me a note telling me that they did and exactly how much.

My mother did all the bookwork for the store. Every Sunday evening, she sat at the dining room table doing all the financials. She balanced everything to the penny every week!

My parents had the store for thirty-two years. When my father passed away, in 1986, my mother ran the store by herself for six months. It was too much for her so she finally retired in 1987. She certainly deserved to retire after how hard she worked her entire life.

My mother and father were amazing people! They worked together in everything they did to provide the best for our family. We never went without the things we needed or even the things we wanted.

"In addition to meatballs and sausage, other meat showed up on our Sunday dinner table. Because we had the store, the meat was usually something that a customer brought to my parents; a squirrel, a rabbit, and an occasional turtle. I always asked what was in the sauce before I would eat it!"

First Memory

Melanie & me, 2006

I enjoy hearing their stories when I ask people to tell me about the first memory in their lives. Some memories go back as far as when they were two years old and others are from grammar school.

My first memory was when I was three and a half years old. I always followed my older brothers around because I didn't have any friends. One day there were three little girls outside that were around my age, cousins of one of their friends. They told me to go play with "the little girls over there." So I did! They became my "second family." I didn't have a sister so they became my sisters. Eventually there were six; Jackie, Bonnie Lynn, Melanie, Laureen, Carrie Ann, and Michelle. Melanie was my first best friend! She was two and a half when we met.

From that day on, we lived our everyday lives together. I slept over and ate dinner at their house all the time. We swam in their swimming pool every day in the summer. At night we caught lightening bugs. I'd go for car rides with their family on Sundays and go out for Friday fish fries and chocolate milk.

At night when it was dark out and time to go home, Melanie and I would walk together to the corner that was the midpoint between our houses. That corner had bushes going in both directions so we couldn't see if there might be someone hiding in them. We always thought someone was there.

XIX

We'd reach the corner and then at the given moment we would run in opposite directions to each of our own houses, yelling all the way so we knew that we both got home safely! One night when we walked together to the corner, Melanie and I thought we saw someone in the bushes. Both of us ran like crazy back to her house, falling in the front door on top of each other and trying to crawl into the house! The memory is fresh in my mind like it was yesterday and it still makes me laugh!

We did all the normal things kids do together and there are some times that stand out in my mind. We used to go trick or treating together every year. We would go to other neighborhoods and get a lot of candy. Back then we got full size candy bars and a lot of them! Jackie and Melanie will never let me forget a time when we went trick or treating when I was about ten years old. I was leaning on the front door after we rang the doorbell. When they opened the door, I fell into the house!

Every Christmas Eve, Melanie and I exchanged gifts and went to each other's houses to see what the other got for Christmas. I remember one year, opening my gift from Melanie, I thought that I had opened the gift I had bought and wrapped up for her. We had bought each other the same soft, warm, cozy white sweater!

Each year, we went to midnight mass for Christmas. Many years we attended the same church. After the service, Melanie, her mother and sisters would come over to my house and the "ladies" would sit at our kitchen table and eat all of the delicious things my mother made for the holidays. It was a special time that we shared for many years!

XX

We have so many wonderful memories. I guess that comes from being friends our whole lives. I don't remember life without all of them in it. They were never just friends, they were family; and my sisters.

We didn't go to the same school until we went to high school at Mount Carmel High School. Melanie and I decided to graduate from high school in three years instead of four. I don't know why we were in such a hurry. To accomplish that goal, we had to go to summer school to get the required classes and credits. We were probably the only two kids that ever went to summer school because we wanted to and our summer school teachers loved us for that reason! We then changed schools and went to East High School for our sophomore year. For our third and final year of high school we went to the newly opened Auburn High School. We were in the first graduating class, the class of 1971.

We went to Auburn Community College together for two years and then to SUNY Oswego, in Oswego, NY, from which we both graduated. After graduating, we went on separate paths but remained close. Through the years we visited each other in almost every city and state where each of us has lived. I visited Melanie and her husband when they were living and working in London, England.

Melanie's sister Laureen was born when we were five years old. When she was five or six years old, she gave my mother a dime for Mother's Day. When Laureen was getting married, my mother gave Laureen that dime at her bridal shower. Laureen still has it!

Carrie Ann and Michele were my "baby sisters." I thought it was fun taking care of them, playing with them, and watching them grow up! I didn't have a baby in my own house. I was the "baby," and I always was my mother's baby no matter how old I was, even when I had babies of my own.

When I began creating the recipes for this book, I asked people which of my mother's recipes they remember. Everyone said something different. Laureen's favorite was Sicilian Broccoli & Beef Pasta, one of the many unique ways my mother cooked pasta.

Growing up with my "second family," I had the opportunity to eat all of the delicious Polish foods that their mother cooked. My favorite was, and still is, kapusta. My "second mother," Rose, used to send home bowls of it with me when I was a young girl and I would eat it for breakfast. It is made with split peas, sauerkraut, one potato, and salt pork and black pepper for flavor. I learned to make this dish many years ago and still make it. I also learned how to make Polish Pigs in the Blanket and Polish Pancakes.

Memories are so precious and wonderful to remember as we grow older.

Sicilian Pasta Fazuli

I grew up eating my mother's Pasta Fazuli, made with dry red kidney beans and pig skin. When I walked in the house after school, I knew what was for dinner. My mother cooked the beans earlier in the day so when I got home they were cooked. I would grab a bowl and fill it with broth and beans. Closer to dinner time, she added the rest of the ingredients.

When I cooked, I always let my kids taste everything every step of the way, just like my mother let me. I guess I am the same kind of mother to my kids that my mother was to me!

When I was in college, I worked at a local Italian restaurant. Their recipe for Pasta Fazuli started with cannelli beans, which gave it a different flavor. I have used both recipes when I made it for my family. My mother's recipe is an authentic Sicilian dish straight from Pozzallo, Sicily. My recipe comes from my home town. Try both recipes and decide which you like more.

Sicilian Cassata

A decadent cake that my aunt, Francesca, made for Christmas is a Sicilian Cassata. On our dinner table there were also dishes of cream puffs, cannoli, ribbon cookies drizzled with honey, and a variety of other delicious Christmas treats. But the Sicilian Cassata stood out with its white ricotta cream, maraschino cherries, toasted almonds, and bits of milk chocolate.

Through the years my aunt told me it was difficult to make! After my mother passed away in 2006, I took home her recipe file box and the recipes for sponge cake and ricotta cream were in it. I decided to tackle it as I was curious to find out how difficult it was to make.

The first thing I did was make the sponge cake following the recipe. It wasn't too difficult. To be sure I could make them, within a week and a half, I made sponge cakes three times! They came out just the way they were supposed to!

Next, I made the ricotta cream following the recipe I found in the box. I measured the milk, sugar, and cornstarch into a large pan. On medium heat, I cooked and whisked the mixture until is started thickening; at least that is what it was supposed to do.

I added the ricotta cheese and the flavorings and continued to stir, still waiting for it to thicken, which it never did. I was ready to throw it out but before I did I called my aunt to ask her advice. She didn't know what I did wrong but she told me to add more cornstarch. So I added more corn starch and continued cooking and stirring until it was thick enough to put on the cake.

I couldn't figure out why, that after following the recipe to a T, it didn't come out right. I took a closer look at the recipe. Instead of writing two cups of milk, my mother had written two quarts of milk! The mystery was solved and now my ricotta cream comes out perfect every time, and yours will too!

Feast of Saint Lucy

Following Sicilian tradition, my mother, Lucia, the first girl born in her family, was supposed to be named Josephine after her paternal grandmother. But when she was born on December 13, 1920, on The Feast of Saint Lucy, or "Santa Lucia," her mother "didn't want to take her name away from her," so she named her Lucia. The second girl born in their family was named Josephine.

The statue of Saint Lucy shows her holding a plate with eyeballs on it. Saint Lucy is the Patron Saint of the Blind or Visually Impaired. In her other hand, she holds a stalk of wheat. There was a severe famine in 1582 and Sicilians believed that Santa Lucia intervened when ships filled with grain came into their harbor on December 13. People were so hungry that they boiled the grain rather than taking the time to grind it into flour. This is how the tradition of eating boiled wheat came to be.

Each year on the Feast Day of Santa Lucia, in Sicily, the people do not eat anything made with wheat flour. Instead, they eat a dish called "cuccia" which is made with boiled wheat, sugar and cream, usually made with ricotta. I make this with our family recipe of Sicilian Cream, the way my mother used to make it.

Every year, on the Feast Day of Santa Lucia, my mother cooked wheat and made Sicilian Cream. She brought bowls of it to her mother and father, her sisters and brothers, and to her aunts and cousins. This was a tradition she enjoyed throughout her life.

In honor of my mother, I make "cuccia" on her birthday. Share our tradition of honoring Santa Lucia, after whom my mother was named.

"On Grandpa Ruta's farm, they grew different kinds of grains. When they harvested the fields, the grain elevator carried the grain into the grain house. As the grain got deeper and deeper, planks were slid into place to make the outside wall taller to hold in the grain. We would jump into the grain, as it filled the grain house, and play with the big green grasshoppers that came in with it."

Table of Contents

Story Pages

Sicilian Green Olives

Green Bean Salad

Salads & Breads

Mom's Green Lettuce Salad

Sicilian Potato Salad

Sunday Morning Oregano Bread

How To Make...

Sunday Morning Oregeno Bread

Lucia, Always The Gardener

Sicilian Green Olives

We always had a bowl of Sicilian Green Olives in our pantry ready to eat whenever we wanted. They were great with lunch or dinner but also to eat with Sicilian bread, cheese, pepperoni, and whatever else we could think of.

My mother used to buy green olives in a large wooden crate. She would prepare them by first hitting them with a hammer to crack them, put them in water, cover them, soak them in a dark place for days, changing the water daily, then can them so we had enough for the whole year. Then she would "fix" them to eat. You can buy Sicilian Green Olives, ready to "fix," in specialty markets.

Ingredients:

1 ½ lb. Whole Sicilian Green Olives, with or without pits
8 cloves fresh garlic cut in large pieces
½ tsp. crushed red pepper
½ tsp. basil
¾ tsp. oregano
3 T. olive oil
2 T. vegetable oil

Directions:

Drain the water from the olives and put in a large covered bowl. Peel and cut up the cloves of garlic and add to olives. Sprinkle olives with the red pepper, basil, and oregano. Drizzle olive oil and vegetable oil over olives. Stir so all the olives are well coated. Store in refrigerator. Stir before serving. You can add bite-size pieces of mozzarella cheese, celery, carrots, hot or sweet peppers, and/or pepperoni, if you'd like. They also go great with Sunday Morning Oregano Bread.

Green Bean Salad

Serves 4

Ingredients:

1 lb. fresh green beans
2 plum tomatoes
2 ½ tsp. olive oil
2 ½ tsp. apple cider vinegar
½ tsp. salt
¼ tsp. pepper

Directions:

Cut the tips off both ends of the green beans. Cut beans in half.

Put the beans in a pan and cover with water. Cover pan. Bring to a boil then turn heat down to medium/low. Cook until they are tender. Drain, cool, and put in a salad bowl.

Cut the plum tomatoes into bite-size pieces. Add them to the green beans.

Sprinkle with salt and pepper. Drizzle the olive oil and vinegar over the beans and tomatoes and stir well.

"On the side of our garage next to the garden, parsley grew, squeezed between the cement sidewalk and the cement wall of the garage."

2

Mom's Green Lettuce Salad

Serves 6

Ingredients:

7 c. iceberg lettuce
1 large tomato
½ of one cucumber, peeled
1 stalk celery

1/8 tsp. salt
1/8 tsp. pepper
5 tsp. apple cider vinegar
6 tsp. olive oil

Directions:

Tear lettuce into large pieces. Cut the vegetables into bite-size pieces. Put into a large salad bowl.

Sprinkle with the salt, pepper, apple cider vinegar and olive oil. Mix well so vegetables are coated with the dressing.

"Every year, my mother, aunt, and grandmother planted a large garden, growing tomatoes, peppers, onions, and other vegetables. They tended the garden together, always wearing aprons. They caught rain water for the garden in a large metal garbage can sitting under a downspout on the house. They used the natural resources that were available."

Two Questions

There are two questions I ask people when the opportunity arises. Their answers have surprised me. They are certainly conversation starters!

The first question is, "If you could eat only one food for the rest of your life, and had to give up everything else, what would that one food be?" My answer is potatoes, which I have loved, cooked any way, throughout my life.

My Nona Ruta made Sicilian Potato Salad for us all of the time. My mother made it for my father, who only liked potato salad made this way. It is a unique and simple recipe, something different than the potato salad everyone else makes.

The second question I like to ask people, who always surprise me with their answers, is, "What is your first memory in your life?" You can read mine in my story, "First Memory," one of the many stories in this book.

"I loved my mother's Sicilian Green Olives and brought them to school. My friend, Diane, brought cheese. Both were very flavorful, to put it mildly! We hid them in our desks. Then, we would lift our desk tops up, stick our heads in our desks, and eat olives and cheese, during classes, of course, until someone screamed out that our food smelled! We were told to put our olives and cheese on the coat rack in the hallway. We weren't allowed to keep our olives and cheese in the classroom!"

Sicilian Potato Salad

Serves 4

Ingredients:

2 lbs. white potatoes cut into large bite-size pieces
1 tsp. salt (put in the water to cook potatoes)

¼ - ½ tsp. salt
¼ - ½ tsp. pepper
½ - ¾ tsp. oregano
1 – 2 T. olive oil
2 - 3 tsp. Apple Cider vinegar

Directions:

Peel the potatoes and cut them into large bite-size pieces. Put in a pan, cover with water, stir in one teaspoon of salt. Bring to a boil on high. When it starts to boil, turn down the temperature to medium and cook until the potatoes are tender but still firm. Do not overcook. Drain the water from the potatoes and put them in a bowl.

Sprinkle the potatoes with ¼ teaspoon salt, ¼ teaspoon pepper, and ½ teaspoon oregano. Drizzle with one tablespoon olive oil and two teaspoons vinegar. Stir gently to mix the ingredients being careful to not break up the potatoes. Add more salt, pepper, oregano, olive oil and vinegar to suit your taste. Serve warm or cold.

Cover and refrigerate leftovers.

Sunday Morning Oregano Bread

As far back as I can remember, every Sunday after church we stopped at the bakery to buy a loaf of warm, fresh-out-of-the-oven Italian bread. When we opened the bakery door, the smell of pastries, cakes, cookies, pies and breads was overwhelming and out of this world!

Sunday was the day of the week that we got to choose something from the bakery, but we had to wait until we got home to eat it. I always chose a chocolate frosted fudge brownie with walnuts on top! I also loved donuts filled with white cream! My father liked peanut covered donuts and enjoyed them dunked in his coffee.

Now back to the bread! We bought one loaf for our Sicilian Sunday Morning Oregano Bread. It was the only day we ate bread "fixed" like this. My mother cut the whole loaf of bread horizontally and laid it out open flat. Then she drizzled olive oil on both sides followed by crushed oregano sprinkled on both sides. She put the halves back together and cut slices for each of us; my father, mother, 2 brothers and me.

My father and I liked Swiss cheese in ours. In those days we didn't have microwaves. We had a gas stove with flame burners. We would put a slice of Swiss cheese on a fork and hold it over the flame to melt but not so long that the cheese would fall onto the burner. Then we would put the cheese into our oregano bread. It was so delicious!

This was a ritual reserved only for Sunday mornings after church.

When I recently spoke to my Aunt Maggie about our Sicilian Sunday Morning Oregano Bread, she told me that she remembered having it when she was growing up on the farm. My grandmother made all the bread they ate so they always had hot bread fresh out of the oven. (This makes my mouth water as I remember eating my grandmother's incredible bread!) They fixed their bread with olive oil and oregano, but they also added anchovies or sardines! If you like, you can add these to your portion of oregano bread as well as olives, hot peppers, or any kind of meat you prefer. Be creative!

This is something simple and delicious that we enjoyed every Sunday morning. Stop at a bakery on a Sunday morning and pick up a loaf of warm, fresh-out-of-the-oven bread and start a new tradition! Maybe you can choose a special pastry too!

What you need:

1 loaf warm fresh Italian bread
Olive oil
Oregano
A variety of cheeses, anchovies, sardines, peppers, olives, meat, and other toppings

How to fix:

Cut the loaf of bread horizontally
Drizzle with olive oil
Sprinkle with oregano
Add other toppings of your choice

Cut and enjoy!

Notes

Nona Ruta's Sicilian Chicken Soup

Soup & More

Sicilian Broccoli & Beef Pasta

Sicilian Sauce with Eggs & Peas

How To Make...

Nona Ruta's Sicilian Chicken Soup

Family

**Grandma & Grandpa
Ruta**

**Pam – Age 3
Cooking Eggs**

Nona Ruta's Sicilian Chicken Soup

On Sunday, my mother, brothers, and I went to "the farm." My aunts, uncles, and cousins were there too. The kitchen was always loud with all of the adults talking, like Sicilians talk; VERY LOUD! Because Nona Ruta was partially deaf, they spoke all the louder for her to hear the conversations. The conversations were spoken half in Sicilian and half in English. I understood our Sicilian dialect because I heard it every day since I was born.

When my kids, Pam and Tommy, were at my parents' house, both Sicilian and English were spoken. They would be hearing a conversation spoken in English, but half way through, it changed to Sicilian. They only understood half of the story! Asking my daughter about it, she said that she was used to it and just never got the end of some stories.

Back to Sundays at the farm! Nona made a huge pot of chicken soup with little meatballs every Sunday. It was so delicious, but when she made it, it was that much more delicious because of her homemade noodles! Noodles at Nona's were always homemade! And, she always sent a large canning jar full of soup home with us.

My Nona's soup was the best! Everything she cooked or baked was delicious! My mother learned to cook from her. I learned from my mother and my children learned from me. Watching me make all of the recipes that were handed down in our family, they know what every dish is and how it should look, smell, and taste. When they want to make something, all they need is a list of ingredients. We still enjoy all of Nona's delicious foods!

9

Nona Ruta's Sicilian Chicken Soup with Little Meatballs

Serves 6

Ingredients:

Water
5 - 6 pounds chicken thighs and legs with skin
2 stalks of celery cut into bite size pieces
½ c. carrots cut into bite size pieces
1 cooking onion (about the size of a baseball) peeled and cut into quarters
¼ c. diced tomatoes
1 ½ tsp. salt
1 - 2 c. of little meatballs made from the meatball recipe
12 oz. fine egg noodles
Grated Pecorino Romano Cheese

Directions:

Make little meatballs using meatball recipe.

Put chicken in a colander and rinse with cold water. Cut off the fat. Put the chicken in a large soup pot and cover with water. Cover pan. Bring to a boil. Skim off the foam that floats on the top of the water.

Add the onion, celery, carrots and tomatoes. Bring to a boil again. Cover pan with lid tilted, leaving a small opening for steam to escape. Lower heat. Simmer for 1 hour.

Add salt and little meatballs to the soup. Add one more cup of hot water. Simmer another half hour.

Remove the chicken from the soup and place in a separate bowl to serve and/or cut up some to put in the soup.

Cook the egg noodles in a separate pan following directions on the package. Drain. Add enough noodles to soup so it is the thickness that you prefer. Add less noodles for a thinner soup with more broth. You can also use home-made noodles, cut thin.

Serve in soup bowls. Sprinkle with Pecorino Romano Cheese.

***Note: Make little meatballs using the meatball recipe. Use about one quarter of the amount the recipe makes. Form meatballs and drop them into the soup to cook. Do not cook them before putting them in the soup. The beef, pork, cheese, seasoned bread crumbs, salt, pepper, and garlic from the meatballs adds additional flavor to the soup.

Use the rest of the meatball mix to make large meatballs. Brown the large meatballs in the oven following meatball baking directions. Cool. Freeze for next time you make sauce.

If you want, you can freeze about a cup full of meatball mix for next time you make soup. I make the mini soup meatballs and freeze them on a cookie sheet. When they are frozen I put them in a freezer bag and save them for next time I make soup!

Sicilian Broccoli and Beef Pasta

Makes 6 servings

Ingredients:

1 T. olive oil
1 ½ c. chopped onion
1 ½ lb. lean ground beef in bite size pieces
5 c. water
5 c. chopped broccoli florets and stems cut into bite size pieces
1 c. diced tomatoes
1 tsp. sugar
1 ½ tsp. garlic powder
1 ½ tsp. salt
¼ tsp. black pepper
4 c. cooked ditalini pasta or home-made pasta

Directions:

Pour olive oil into a large soup pan. Sauté onions. Add ground beef and cook until browned. Add the water and bring to a boil. Add the broccoli, tomatoes, sugar, garlic powder, salt and pepper. Put a lid on the pan, tilted for steam to escape. Reduce heat to low and simmer for about half an hour or until broccoli is tender.

Cook ditalini following package directions. Drain and measure four cups. Add to beef and broccoli soup. Add water, half cup at a time, if you want more broth, or add less ditalini. Add more ditalini if you want it thicker.

Aprons & A Little Kitchen

Sicilian Sauce with Hardboiled Eggs & Peas is a meatless dish that is easy to prepare in a short time. It is served on pasta. Being Catholic, it was a nice meal on a Friday as we didn't eat meat.

My grandmother brought this dish with her from Siculiana, Sicily, to America. My aunt, Francesca, is who made this dish. I can still see her standing at her stove, all 5 feet tall and 95 pounds of her, wearing one of the many colorful aprons that she used to make. She made aprons for everyone including my mother and me. When I was about five years old, she made me a light blue apron and a pretty green one, both having rick-rack around the top and rick-rack framing a little pocket.

My aunt Francesca lived upstairs from us with her mother and father. They had a little stove in their back kitchen on which they cooked everything. Most Sicilians have two kitchens and I never saw my aunt or grandmother cook in their larger kitchen on the large stove.

Sicilian Sauce with Hardboiled Eggs & Peas is a combination of foods that you wouldn't think go together, but they do and they taste delicious! It isn't a fancy dish but rather something that would be eaten during the week. Make it for family and friends so they can experience a unique dish that they have never before tasted!

Sicilian Sauce with Eggs & Peas

Serves 3 or 4

Ingredients:

1 tsp. olive oil
1 large clove garlic, minced
1 (15 oz.) can tomato sauce
1 (6 oz.) can tomato paste
2 ½ (6 oz.) cans of water
¼ tsp. baking soda

2 ½ tsp. sugar
1/8 tsp. salt
1/8 tsp. pepper
1 c. frozen/canned peas
3 or 4 peeled hardboiled eggs
8 - 12 oz. pasta of your choice
Grated Parmesan cheese

Directions:

Place eggs in a pan with water covering them. Bring to a boil. Lower heat and cook for 10 minutes. Drain water.

Measure olive oil into a medium sauce pan. Sauté' garlic. Add tomato paste and tomato sauce. Stir until it is smooth. Measure the water in the tomato paste can and add to the sauce. Stir. Add baking soda, sugar, salt and pepper and stir. Cover pan, tilt cover for steam to escape. Simmer on low for 30 minutes. If the sauce is bitter, stir in another quarter teaspoon baking soda and half teaspoon sugar. Add peeled eggs to the sauce. Simmer 10 minutes on low. Add peas. Cook for 5 minutes, just long enough to heat them up.

Cook pasta following package directions. Drain. Ladle sauce and one egg over each serving of pasta. Sprinkle with Parmesan cheese.

**Sicilian Sausage,
Peppers, Onions
& Potatoes**

Beef Cutlets

**Sicilian Sunday
Sauce with Meat**

Sauces & Main Dish
Meat & Fish

Meatballs

Bracioli

Octopus

How To Make...

Bracioli

Sunday Sauce with Meat

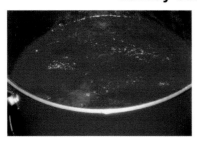 

Sunday At The Farm

When we visited my grandparents on their farm each Sunday afternoon, my grandmother would be standing at the stove cooking. Nona Ruta was a short, round little lady with her gray hair always gathered into a low bun on the back of her head. She always wore a dress that went down past her knees and it was always covered by an apron. She wore heavy thick gray or black stockings and black shoes that were "old ladyish." This is how I saw my grandmother when I was a little girl and it is how I remember her now.

On some of those Sundays she cooked Sicilian Sausage, Peppers, Onions, and Potatoes for all of our family gathered around her kitchen table. Nona Ruta also made homemade bread. The smells of the sausage, peppers, onions, and potatoes cooking on the stove and her homemade bread baking in the oven filled every corner of the farm house. We couldn't wait to feast on her delicious creations! She was an amazing lady and everything she cooked was delicious! When I make this dish my kitchen smells as wonderful as my Nona's farm house!

"In the winter, the snow drifts were so high at the farm that we could climb up onto the roof of the chicken coop and jump off into the deep snow. It was a wonder none us were ever buried in it. We always had fun at the farm!"

Sicilian Sausage, Peppers, Onions, & Potatoes

Serves 6

Ingredients:

1 1/2 lb. Italian Sausage; pork, chicken or turkey, hot or mild, in casings or patties
½ c. water
2 large sweet onions, peeled and cut into strips
4 large green peppers, cut into strips
2 medium to large potatoes
½ tsp.salt
¼ tsp. pepper
Crushed Red Pepper (optional)

Directions:

Squeeze sausage out of casings and break up into bite-size pieces or break sausage patties into bite-size pieces. Put in a large pan and add ½ cup of water. On medium, cook sausage, stirring, until it is browned. Add onions to sausage and cook for about 5 minutes. Stir in the green peppers. Cover the pan and simmer for 15 minutes.

Add salt and black pepper. Add the potatoes, stirring them in so they are covered with the sausage, peppers and onions. Turn heat down to low so it is a gentle boil. Cover the pan with lid tilted for steam to escape and simmer until the peppers are soft and the potatoes are cooked but still firm, about 10 minutes. Serve in soup bowls or on bread.

Beef Cutlets

Beef cutlets are a main dish my mother made that was delicious served with salad, mashed potatoes and a vegetable.

Preheat oven 350 degrees
Total baking time, 30 minutes
Spray baking pan with non-stick cooking spray

Ingredients:

1 lb. cube steak cut into 4 or 6 portions
2 c. Italian Seasoned bread crumbs
¼ tsp. salt
¼ tsp. pepper

1 tsp. parsley
1/8 tsp. garlic powder

3 eggs, beaten
¼ tsp. salt
1/8 tsp. pepper

Olive oil

Directions:

Mix bread crumbs, ¼ teaspoon salt, ¼ teaspoon pepper, parsley, and garlic powder in a large bowl. Set aside.

Mix the beaten eggs with ¼ teaspoon salt and 1/8 teaspoon pepper.

Dip each piece of meat in the egg mixture coating both sides. Next, put each in bread mixture and coat on each side. Place cutlets on a baking sheet with low sides. Drizzle olive oil on both sides. Bake for about 14 minutes, turn over and bake 10 minutes, or until both sides are golden brown.

Breaded Pork Chops

Serves 4
Preheat oven 350 degrees
Spray a baking sheet with non-stick cooking spray

Ingredients:

4 pork chops, about 6 oz. each
2 cups Italian Style Bread Crumbs
Dash of salt
Dash of pepper
2 eggs
Olive oil

Directions:

Break eggs into a shallow bowl. Add a dash of salt and pepper. Beat with a fork to mix well.

Place bread crumbs in a shallow bowl. Add a dash of salt and pepper to the breadcrumbs and mix well.

Dip a pork chop in the egg mixture and coat well on both sides. Next, put the pork chop in the breadcrumbs and coat well on both sides. Place the pork chop on the baking sheet. Repeat with all of the pork chops. Drizzle olive oil on both sides of the pork chops.

Bake for 20 minutes. Turn them over and bake for another 15 minutes, or until both sides are browned.

Meat for Sauce

Serves 6

Prepare your choice of meat for Sicilian Sunday Sauce with Meat (Page 26), or Simple Everyday Sicilian Sauce (Page 28).

2 or 3 meatballs per person (Recipe on page 21)
Bracioli (Recipe on page 22)
6 – 8 links hot or mild sausage; pork, chicken, or turkey (Cooking directions below)
1 ½ lbs. beef, cut into 3 inch squares (Cooking directions below)
½ c. water
1 T. olive oil

Directions:

Make Meatballs and/or bracioli.

To cook sausage: Cut sausage links in half. Pierce sausage with a fork on all sides. Put the sausage in a frying pan with half cup of water. Cover pan. Cook on medium heat, browning on all sides. Add more water if it evaporates.

To cook beef: Put oil in a frying pan and warm it up on medium heat. Add the beef and cook until it is browned on all sides.

The meatballs, bracioli, sausage, and beef will finish cooking in the sauce.

Leftover sauce with meat freezes well in a freezer container. You can also freeze the meat that you cooked, but did not put in the sauce, for the next time you make sauce.

Making Meatballs & Memories

I made meatballs with my mother, Lucy, ever since I was a little girl. Every Saturday, when my mother was making meatballs for Sunday, I grated the dried loaf of Italian bread and a large triangular piece of Pecorino Romano cheese, scratching my fingers on the grater as the bread and cheese became smaller. My mother had already ground the beef, pork and veal. Everything my mother made, she made from scratch. She made her own sausage, grinding the meat in an old fashioned, crank-handled grinder, then filling the casings by hand.

Each and every Sunday at noon we had pasta with sauce, meatballs, sausage, and beef all made from scratch. We would sometimes find "other meats" in the sauce including rabbits, squirrels, and an occasional turtle.

I loved helping my mother in the kitchen. My mother made all of her wonderful dishes by smell and taste. Spending years with her, cooking and baking, I learned those smells and tastes so I could make them to taste just like hers.

Everyone loved my mother's meatballs! My children would only eat the meatballs their grandmother and I made! My mother made meatballs and sauce throughout her life. She probably made meatballs every week for 80 years!

Meatballs made from my mother's recipe are the most delicious and tender you will ever taste!

Meatballs

Preheat oven to 350 degrees
Makes about 25
Spray baking sheet with non-stick cooking spray

Ingredients:

1 ¼ lb. ground beef
½ lb. ground pork
2 ½ c. Italian Style bread crumbs
½ tsp. salt
½ tsp. black pepper
½ tsp. garlic powder
or 1 tsp. minced garlic

1 T. parsley flakes
½ c. Pecorino Romano cheese
5 extra-large eggs
¼ c. water
½ c. milk

Directions:

Put the beef, pork, and veal (you can substitute ½ lb. veal for ½ lb. of the beef) in a large bowl. Add bread crumbs, salt, pepper, garlic, and parsley. Mix. Add the eggs, water and milk. Mix well. Shape meatballs and place on a cookie sheet that has low sides.

Bake in pre-heated oven for 15 minutes or until browned. Turn over meatballs and bake 10 minutes. Turn again and bake until meatballs are browned on all sides. Meatballs will finish cooking in the sauce.

They freeze well for a future meal. You can also make little meatballs for Nona Ruta's Chicken Soup, freeze them on a cookie sheet, and put in a freezer bag after they are frozen.

Bracioli

Preheat oven 350 degrees
Serves 4 – 6
Spray baking sheet with non-stick cooking spray

Ingredients:

3 bottom round steaks sliced very thin and about a 4" x 6" rectangle each (about ¾ lb. total)

1 lb. ground meatball mix; any combination of beef, pork, and veal
1 c. Italian seasoned bread crumbs
¼ c. Pecorino Romano cheese
½ tsp. garlic powder or 1 tsp. fresh garlic, minced
¼ tsp. salt
¼ tsp. pepper
½ tsp. parsley
2 raw eggs
¼ c. milk
15 thin slices pepperoni cut into small pieces
3 hard-boiled eggs, cut into pieces

Directions:

To make filling, put the beef/pork/veal, bread crumbs, Pecorino Romano cheese, salt, pepper, and garlic powder in a large bowl. Mix well. Add the raw eggs and milk. Mix together, put in the pepperoni pieces and mix again.

Divide the filling into three portions, one for each steak. Lay out one of the thin steaks. Save 1/3 of the portion of filling to put on top of hard-boiled egg pieces. Put the larger amount of filling on the right edge of the steak, width-wise edge to edge, and flatten it out a little. Put pieces of one hard-boiled egg on the filling. Put the 1/3 portion of the filling on top of the eggs and wrap it around the egg pieces. Starting from the right side, roll the steak around the filling until you reach the left end.

Cut a long piece of kitchen string. Starting on one end, wrap the string around the bracioli until you reach the other end then wrap going back to where you started. Tie ends together.

Repeat with each steak.

Place the bracioli on a cookie sheet that has low sides. Bake for 15 minutes. Turn them over and bake another 12 minutes. They will finish cooking in the sauce.

Shopping On a Budget

A dish that my mother sometimes made for dinner when we didn't have pasta was breaded pork chops. Other meals included beef cutlets, baked chicken, chili, or meatloaf. We always had a salad, vegetables and mashed potatoes to go with them. But four nights a week we ate pasta!

You might think these meals cost more than pasta meals but potatoes were inexpensive and chili and meatloaf went a long way. They were made with ground chuck steak which was inexpensive.

Every Thursday morning, when I was a little girl, I loved going grocery shopping with my mother. The grocery store sale ads were in Wednesday night's newspaper and my mother made a list of which stores had the best prices. We always went to four stores. My mother always shopped with coupons and the stores had stamp books. We would get blue stamps for each dollar we spent and then we could use them to get free items such as blankets, toasters and clocks. There were even free drinking glasses in boxes of clothes detergents and the gas stations would give out free cups or drinking glasses if you bought a certain amount of gas!

We returned soda bottles to get our bottle deposit back. We took the bottles up to a window where a person took them and gave us the money.

So vivid in my mind is the memory of my mother and I going to the check-out line where she would find items in the grocery cart that she didn't put in it. She would say, "Where'd this come from?" I would always reply, "It's mine, Mommy."

I would be sitting in the cart and when she wasn't looking, I would take something that I wanted off of a shelf and put it in the cart. Most times, she would buy it for me!

I remember that when we got home from grocery shopping I looked into the bags and said, out loud, "There's nothing to eat." We didn't have ready-to-eat foods. What we bought were the ingredients to make meals. Sometimes we bought potato chips, a box of cookies, or soda. What stands out in my mind is that we came home with a lot of full brown paper bags and it seemed like we got a lot for our money!

Times have certainly changed! As an adult raising my own family, I remember spending what I considered to be a lot of money and coming home with only a few bags of groceries. Now the adult, I get home from the grocery store, look into the bags and think, "There's nothing to eat! And I am doing the shopping!"

There are a lot of ways to save money when shopping. Everything eventually goes on sale. That is when I shop. It's fun to find a bargain!

"When I was a little girl, one of my best friends was Angela. We spent many hours together at her house or mine. Her grandpa would come to pick her up and Angela would always say, "I want to stay longer. Pick me up later." And he would! Her grandparents adored her. I have so many wonderful and precious memories. Angela passed away the summer after sixth grade and I want her to always be remembered."

Sicilian Sunday Sauce with Meat

See **"Meat for Sauce,"** (Page 19) and prepare meatballs, bracioli, or other meat for your sauce. You can put in whatever you want and it can be different every time!

Serves 5 - 6

Ingredients for sauce:

2 T. olive oil
2 tsp. garlic, minced
1 (12 oz.) can tomato paste
1 (29 oz.) can tomato sauce
1 (29 oz.) can tomato puree
2 (12 oz.) cans of water

½ tsp. baking soda
3 - 8 tsp. sugar
½ tsp. crushed basil
½ tsp. salt
½ tsp. black pepper

1 ½ lb. pasta of your choice

Directions:

In a large saucepan sauté the minced garlic in the olive oil over medium heat for about three minutes. Stir so it doesn't burn. Add the tomato paste, tomato puree, tomato sauce and water. Stir until everything is well blended and smooth. Bring to a boil and stir so it doesn't stick to the bottom of the pan. Turn down heat to low.

Add baking soda, basil, salt and pepper. Add the sugar, starting with 3 or 4 teaspoons, and add more until it is the sweetness you prefer. Simmer with the lid tilted open for steam to escape for half an hour. Stir after fifteen minutes so sauce doesn't stick to the bottom of the pan.

Add your choice of meat; meatballs, sausage, bracioli, and/or beef. Turn heat to medium and cook until it starts to boil, then turn down to low. Cover with the lid tilted open and simmer for an hour and a half stirring every twenty minutes. If it appears to be too thick add an extra half can of water at any time while it simmers.

Cook pasta following directions on the package. When the pasta is cooked, drain it in a colander. Put it back into the pan and stir some sauce into it so it doesn't stick together. Serve on dinner plates or large soup bowls. Extra sauce and grated Pecorino Romano Cheese sprinkled on top are nice additions.

Take the meat out of the sauce and put it in a bowl to serve at the table.

My parents always had a little glass of burgundy wine with dinner!

Simple Everyday Sicilian Sauce

Ingredients:

1 T. olive oil
½ tsp. minced garlic
1 (12 oz.) can tomato paste
1 ½ c. water
1 (28 oz.) can crushed tomatoes
¼ tsp. baking soda
6 tsp. sugar

½ tsp. salt
1/4 tsp. black pepper
¼ tsp. basil
½ tsp. parsley
Meatballs, sausage, bracioli

Directions:

In a large saucepan, sauté garlic in olive oil for 1 minute on medium heat. Add the tomato paste and water. Stir until it is blended and smooth. Add the crushed tomatoes and stir. Stir in the baking soda, sugar, salt, black pepper, basil, and parsley. Add additional sugar later if you want a sweeter sauce. Bring to a slow boil. Turn heat to low and simmer for half an hour with the cover tilted open for steam to escape. Stir in 15 minutes so it doesn't stick to the pan. Add the meat of your choice to the sauce. Simmer on low for 1 1/2 hours with cover tilted open. Stir every half hour.

Cook pasta following package directions. Drain and serve with sauce and meat.

Octopus

It is a custom for Sicilians to not eat meat on Christmas Eve. Octopus is one of the foods we always had on our dinner table in addition to squid, fried cod fish, snails, Sicilian Covered Pizza, and cheese pizza. We finished our meal with Sicilian pastries, desserts, cookies and espresso coffee.

One octopus serves about 2 people for a main dish or 3 – 4 as an appetizer.

Ingredients:

1 octopus, fresh or frozen, about 1 ½ lbs.
1 tsp. olive oil
½ tsp. vinegar
Dash of salt
Dash of pepper

Directions:

Rinse the octopus with cool water. If it is frozen, cover with water in a pan and let it thaw out. Change the water a couple times. You can start cooking it before it thaws completely.

Cover the octopus with water in a large pan. Bring to a boil. Lower temperature and simmer for approximately half an hour. It needs to cook long enough so it is not tough. You can cut a small piece off and taste it to make sure it is cooked enough.

When it is cooked, drain the water and put the octopus in a bowl. Cut it into bite-size pieces. Drizzle with olive oil and vinegar, and sprinkle with salt and pepper. Mix well. Eat hot or cold. Store leftovers in refrigerator.

Fried Cod Fish

Cod fish, in Sicilian, is "Baccala." It is one of the foods Sicilians eat on Christmas Eve when we do not eat meat.

Serves 4

Ingredients:

1 ½ lb. of Cod Fish (Preserved in salt)
¾ c. flour
¼ tsp. salt
1/8 tsp. black pepper
¼ tsp. parsley, finely crushed
2/3 c. milk
1/3 c. vegetable oil

Directions:

Place cod fish in a large bowl and cover with cold water. Cover the bowl with plastic wrap, place in refrigerator, and soak for 24 to 48 hours. Change the water every 4 hours and return to refrigerator. Dip your finger in the water before each water change and taste to see if all the salt is gone. This will take at least 24 hours. When all the salt has been removed, pat the cod dry with paper towels and cut into 3" x 4" pieces.

Put milk into a shallow bowl.

Put flour in a shallow bowl. Add the salt and pepper. Crush the parsley with your fingers to make it fine and add to flour. Mix well.

To coat cod fish:

Dip a piece of cod in the milk. Next, place it in the flour mixture and spoon some of the flour on top of it. Press the flour into it. Turn it over and repeat until cod is well coated. Dip the flour coated cod in the milk again. Repeat this with all pieces of cod fish.

On high, heat up the oil in a large frying pan. Turn it down to medium. As you coat each piece of cod, place it in the frying pan. Fry it until it is lightly browned on both sides. Add more oil if necessary.

After you have lightly browned all of the pieces of cod, turn the heat down to low and cover the pan. Let it fry slowly until it is a medium brown. Turn over and brown the other side until it is also a medium brown. The coating should be a little crispy.

As each piece is finished frying, remove it to a plate. The fried cod should not be greasy. If there is oil on it, pat it with a paper towel.

Serve hot. If desired, you can squeeze the juice of fresh lemon on it.

"In December, my father sold Christmas trees that he cut down. He stood them up in front of our store where people could choose their perfect Christmas tree. One Christmas, he brought home a small Christmas tree for me! I set it up in my bedroom, at the end of my bed, and decorated it. It is a memory that warms my heart each holiday season when I see Christmas trees for sale."

Notes

Homemade Pasta

All Pastas Are Not The Same

Pasta with Ricotta

Main Dish Pasta

Sicilian Ricotta Filled Ravioli

Sicilian Baked Macaroni

Sicilian Lasagna

Lucia's Pasta Fazuli

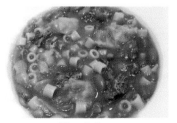

Maria's Pasta Fazuli

Sicilian Pasta con Sarde

How To Make...

Homemade Pasta

Sicilian Ricotta Filled Ravioli

 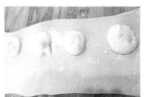

Sicilian Baked Macaroni

Homemade Pasta

There is nothing better than homemade pasta! My mother and my grandmother had three-foot-square pasta boards to roll out their dough and these boards covered half of their tabletops! Their husbands made their boards for them. They also made three-foot-long rolling pins for them out of wooden broomsticks. They could roll out pieces of pasta dough as large as their pasta boards!

They would roll the dough around the rolling pin and unroll it accordion like into layers about four inches wide. Then they would cut the long folded edges on both long sides of their folded dough. So now they had layers of pasta dough, each four inches wide and sometimes almost three feet long.

My mother's sister, Margaret, said that my grandmother would get a very large sharp knife to cut the pasta. As she held it in one hand, she would run the fingers of her other hand down the dough as she cut it. Margaret said that she did it so fast that she thought her mother would cut her fingers! But, she never did!

After she cut the pasta noodles, she would separate them and lay them on a large cotton cloth on her bed to dry before cooking them. My mother did that. I do that, and so does my daughter, Pam. It's just the way we've always done it.

Homemade Pasta

Makes about 1 1/3 pounds of pasta dough

Makes 4 - 5 servings of wide noodles or
enough thin sliced noodles for Sicilian Chicken Soup

Ingredients

3 c. flour + more to roll out dough
1 c. warm water
2 eggs
1 tsp. salt for cooking pasta

Directions:

Measure the flour and put into a large bowl. Add the eggs
and ½ cup of the water and mix by hand or with an electric
mixer on low using the dough hook. Continue adding water
until you have a dough that isn't sticky and forms a ball. If
it is a little sticky, add a little more flour and continue
mixing.

Separate large ball of dough into three smaller
balls. Cover them with plastic wrap so they don't dry out
while you are rolling out each individual ball of dough.

Sprinkle dough board with flour. Place a ball of dough on
the floured dough board and sprinkle flour on it. Start
rolling out the dough from the center going out to the
edges. As you roll the dough, pick it up as it gets larger and
turn it making sure

it isn't sticking to the board. Sprinkle additional flour on the board and on the dough as you continue to roll it out. Roll each ball into a circle about 16 inches round and as thin as you can. Let it dry for about half an hour before cutting it.

Cut the 16-inch circle of dough into 4 inch strips. Stack the strips on top of each other. With a sharp knife, starting at one end, cut the pasta into 1/8-inch-wide strips for soup noodles or 1/2-inch-wide strips for noodles with sauce or other toppings. Repeat this with the other balls of pasta dough.

Separate the slices of pasta, lay them on a cotton towel, and let them dry for a couple hours before cooking. You can cook it soon afterwards or you can cook it within a couple days. You do not need to cover or bag it.

To cook noodles:

Fill a large pan about ¾ full with water and add one teaspoon of salt. Bring to a boil. Put in the pasta and stir it so it separates. Lower heat to a slow boil.

Cook soup noodles for about 5 minutes. Always cook soup noodles in water, separate from the soup broth. Drain and add to Nona Ruta's Sicilian Chicken Soup with Little Meatballs, Pasta with Broccoli & Beef, or Pasta Fazuli.

Cook wide noodles about 10 minutes. Drain water from noodles. Serve wide homemade pasta with Sicilian Sunday Sauce, Pasta with Ricotta, or other toppings of your choice.

Pasta with Ricotta

This is a very simple but tasty way to serve pasta that you can make in minutes. Unless you are Sicilian or know someone who is, you probably have never heard of or tasted pasta served this way.

Serves 4 – 6

Ingredients:

1 lb. pasta noodles, any shape you like
8 oz. ricotta cheese, whole milk or part-skim
Hot water from the pasta
Black pepper
Pecorino Romano Cheese

Directions:

Cook pasta following package directions.

While pasta is cooking, put the ricotta cheese in a bowl. Add hot water from the cooking pasta to the ricotta cheese starting with a couple tablespoons. Stir in. Add more hot water to the ricotta one spoon at a time until it is smooth and creamy but not soupy. It should still be thick enough so that it sticks to the pasta.

When the pasta is cooked, drain it. Serve in pasta bowls. Ladle the ricotta over the pasta. Sprinkle with black pepper and Pecorino Romano Cheese.

Fried Spaghetti

Have you ever had fried spaghetti? My father used to reheat Sunday leftovers this way. We didn't have microwaves so everything had to be reheated on the stove in a pan. Frying the spaghetti in olive oil gives it a different flavor and texture than pasta with sauce that hasn't been fried. It is really delicious!

Directions:

Put about a tablespoon of olive oil in a frying pan. Add leftover spaghetti, or other leftover pasta, with sauce on it. Cut up leftover meatballs and pieces of sausage and add them to the pasta.

On medium/high heat, continuously stir the pasta and meat so it doesn't stick to the bottom of the pan and burn. Fry it until it is hot and a little crusty.

Sprinkle with Pecorino Romano Cheese.

"Basil grew out of the cement walls that were the foundation of our garage. Flowers also grew in places that seemed impossible. Seeds from the flowers that grew the year before would fly in the wind or be carried by birds so marigolds, violets, and snapdragons grew randomly in cracks in the sidewalks and the blacktop driveway around our house."

Sicilian Ricotta Filled Ravioli

Impress your guests with home-made ravioli served with Sicilian Sunday Sauce, meatballs, and Italian sausage.

Makes about 32

Ingredients for dough:

3 c. flour
2 eggs
1 c. warm water

Ingredients for Ricotta Filling:

2 c. ricotta cheese
2 eggs
2 T. grated Pecorino Romano Cheese
¼ tsp. salt and a sprinkle of pepper

Directions for dough:

Measure flour into a large bowl. Make a well in the middle and put in eggs. Beat the eggs with a spoon, then mix with the flour. Add water, starting with 1/2 cup, and mix in. Continue to add water a little at a time, enough to form a dough that you can make into a smooth ball that is not sticky. Separate the ball of dough into 3 smaller balls. Set aside.

Directions for Ricotta Filling:

Stir the ingredients for the ricotta filling together thoroughly. Set aside.

Directions for making ravioli:

Sprinkle flour on dough board. Place one of the dough balls in the middle and sprinkle with flour. Starting from the center of the dough, roll outward with a rolling pin. Continue to roll from the middle to shape it into a 9" x 12" rectangle. After it starts getting larger pick it up with the rolling pin, dust the surface with flour again, turn the dough and put it down on the flour. Sprinkle flour on top of the dough and continue to roll until it is very thin. With a wheel cutter, trim off the uneven edges so you have straight edges on all sides. Then cut the dough lengthwise in half.

Make ravioli with one strip at a time. Put 1 tablespoon of ricotta filling on the right side of the dough about 2 inches apart. Fold the left side of the dough over the ricotta filled side. Press the edges with a fork to seal them. Cut each square apart and seal the other edges of each ravioli. You can trim the edges of the ravioli if they are too wide. Leave them ¼ to ½ inch wide. Put the trimmed off dough with the other dough to roll out to make more ravioli. Continue making ravioli until you have used all the dough. Lay them on a cookie sheet covered with parchment paper. Let them dry for about half an hour before cooking. You can also freeze them on the cookie sheet and when they are frozen, put them in freezer bags. Do not thaw out before cooking.

Directions for cooking ravioli:

Fill a large pan with water. Add ½ teaspoon salt. Bring to a boil. Gently place the ravioli in the pan, a few at a time, and turn down the heat so it is a slow boil. If they boil too hard, the ravioli will break apart in the water. Cook for 15 minutes. Remove them with a slotted spoon and put in a colander. Make sure all water drains off. Serve with sauce.

Sicilian Baked Macaroni

When I tell people about my Sicilian Baked Macaroni, they think of baked ziti, never having heard of my family's recipe. It is layers of pasta, sauce, meatballs, eggs, and cheese. It is a recipe that came from Pozzallo, Sicily and it can't be found in any restaurant. It is truly unique!

Pre-heat oven to 350 degrees
Serves 6 or more
9 ½" x 13" Roasting pan
Non-stick cooking spray

Ingredients:

One recipe of Sunday Sauce
6 - 8 home-made meatballs
(or one jar of your favorite sauce and store-bought meatballs for my "cheater recipe")

1 ½ lb. cut ziti or rigatoni pasta
6 oz. sliced pepperoni cut into smaller pieces
5 c. Sunday Sauce
6 – 8 meatballs cut into bite-sized pieces
4 raw eggs
4 oz. shredded mozzarella cheese
6 hard-boiled eggs – peeled and sliced
Pecorino Romano cheese

Directions:

Cook the ziti or rigatoni pasta according to package directions. Drain well. Return to pan. Add 3 ½ cups of the

Sunday Sauce and the pepperoni and stir well. Add the 4 raw eggs and stir in. Add the cut up meatballs and 2 oz. mozzarella cheese and stir in gently.

Spray the bottom of the roasting pan with non-stick cooking spray. For the first layer, spread 1/4 cup of sauce on the bottom of the pan. Spread half of the pasta mix on the bottom of the pan. Spread half cup of sauce over the pasta mix. Spread three of the sliced hard-boiled eggs on top of the sauce and then half of the mozzarella cheese. Sprinkle with Pecorino Romano Cheese.

Spread the rest of the pasta mix on top of the first layer. Spread the other three sliced eggs on top. Cover with half cup of sauce. Next, spread with the rest of the mozzarella cheese and then sprinkle with Pecorino Romano Cheese. Pour about a quarter cup of water around the edges of the layers of pasta to keep it moist while it bakes.

Cover. Bake for 1 hour. Remove from oven. Let it set for about 10 – 15 minutes before serving. Cut baked macaroni into squares. The raw eggs hold it together. Pieces will come out in one piece after it sets for a little while after baking.

Baked macaroni tastes great warmed up the next day!

Sicilian Lasagna

Our Sicilian Lasagna recipe has so much more flavor than others' recipes. We put meatballs in ours. Meatballs have the flavors of all of their ingredients which includes beef, pork, Italian seasoned bread crumbs, Pecorino Romano Cheese, parsley, and garlic.

Preheat oven 350 degrees
9" x 13" Baking dish
Non-stick spray
Serves 6

Ingredients:

12 lasagna noodles
5 c. sauce, home-made (or bought)
8 meatballs, sliced, then cut into pieces
4 c. ricotta cheese, whole milk or part skim
1 T. sugar
3 c. shredded Mozzarella cheese, whole milk or part skim
3 T. grated Pecorino Romano cheese

Directions:

Make sauce and meatballs following recipe directions. (You can make my cheater version using store bought sauce and meatballs.)

Cook meatballs in the sauce. If you use store-bought meatballs, they are smaller, so you will need about a dozen.

Mix ricotta and 1 tablespoon sugar. Set aside. Slice the meatballs and then cut them into smaller pieces. Set aside.

Cook lasagna noodles following directions on the package. Drain noodles in a colander, rinse with cool water, and put back in the pan.

Spray the bottom of the baking dish with non-stick spray. Cover bottom with half cup of sauce. Line bottom of pan with lasagna noodles, overlapping the edges.

Spread 2 cups of the ricotta on the lasagna. Spread 1 ½ cup shredded Mozzarella cheese on the ricotta layer. Next, spread half of the pieces of meatballs on top of the cheese and cover with 1 ½ cups of sauce.

Add another layer of lasagna noodles, then layers of 2 cups ricotta, 1 ½ cup Mozzarella cheese, the rest of the meatballs, and then cover with 1 ½ cups of sauce.

Add a third layer of lasagna noodles and top off with 1 ½ cups of sauce.

Cover with aluminum foil and bake for 45 minutes. Uncover. Sprinkle top with Pecorino Romano cheese and bake for another 10 minutes uncovered. Take it out of the oven and let it set for 10 minutes before serving.

Sicilian Pasta Fazuli

"Lucia's Recipe"

Serves 4 – 6

Ingredients:

1 lb. dry red kidney or Great Northern beans
Water
1 tsp. salt
¾ tsp. pepper
1½ c. chopped onions
3 lb. pig skin and ham/pork cut into large pieces from a
"pork picnic half"
¾ lb. Ditalini pasta or home-made pasta
Crushed Red Pepper (optional)

Directions:

Put dry beans in a large pan and cover with water. Soak
dry beans for 2 hours. Drain water. Add water to about 2
inches above the level of the beans.

On high heat, bring to a boil. When it starts to boil, turn
heat down to low and simmer for 45 minutes or until beans
are tender. Check and stir occasionally. If water gets low,
add 1 cup more and stir in. Bring to a boil again, turn down
heat to low and keep simmering. Add water, a half of a cup
at a time, so it is soupy and the flavor is not watered down.

Add the onion, pig skin and pork. If they are cold when you put them in, let the beans come to a slow boil again and then turn the temperature to low and simmer, with the lid tilted open for steam to escape, for 45 minutes or until the meat is cooked well. Add the salt and pepper.

Cook the pasta separately following package directions. Drain the water and add about half of the pasta to the beans and broth in the pan. It should be a thick soup. Add more until it is the consistency that you like.

Serve in bowls. Sprinkle with Crushed Red Pepper Flakes. (optional)

"It was 1927 when my mother, Lucia, with her mother, Maria, came to America. My mother saved all of the paperwork that was required to enter the country, which included immunization records, one passport for both of them, and identification papers for when they lived here. In all of the legal papers, my grandmother was identified as Maria Campanella, daughter of Salvatore. When they were processed at Ellis Island, my grandmother's name was changed to Mary Ruta. My mother's name changed to Lucy when she entered elementary school."

Sicilian Pasta Fazuli

"Maria's Recipe"

Serves 4 – 6

Ingredients:

1 T. olive oil
1 c. diced yellow onion
3 (19 oz.) cans Cannellini Beans
3 1/2 c. water
1/8 tsp. pepper
1/8 tsp. garlic powder
1 ½ lb. boneless pork, ham, or pig skin
½ of a small head of cabbage
1 T. crushed tomatoes or diced tomatoes

1 lb. pasta – Ditalini or another small pasta of your choice
Sauce (optional)
Crushed Red Pepper (optional)

Directions:

Measure oil into large pan. On medium heat sauté diced onions until transparent, about 4 minutes. Turn heat up to high. Add Cannellini beans and 2 cups water. Cover pan and heat until it starts to boil. Tilt cover so steam escapes. On low heat, simmer for 30 minutes. Stir in the additional 1 1/2 cup of water.

Cut the meat into 4 or 5 large pieces. Turn heat to medium/high and add the meat. When it starts to boil, lower temperature and simmer for 15 minutes.

Cut the cabbage into 3 - 4 wedges, add to the beans and meat, raise to medium/high again. When it comes to a boil reduce to low and cook until the cabbage is soft, about 10 – 15 minutes.

Remove the meat and cabbage from the beans and put in a serving bowl. Serve meat and cabbage on the side or cut up some to put into the pasta fazuli.

Cook pasta according to directions. Drain pasta when it is cooked and add it to the beans, enough so it still is a thick soup. You can add more pasta or less, whichever you prefer.

Serve in bowls topped with a tablespoon of sauce and crushed red pepper. (both optional)

Sicilian Pasta con Sarde

Sicilian Pasta con Sarde is a unique Sicilian dish that is made with sardines, fennel, capers and a blend of spices that together create a delicious flavor! If you like sardines, you will love this dish as much as I do.

Serves 4

Ingredients:

1 tsp. olive oil
1 tsp. minced garlic
1 (6 oz.) can tomato paste
2 (6 oz.) cans water
1 (15 oz.) can tomato sauce
1/8 tsp. baking soda
½ tsp. sugar
1 (8 1/2 oz.) can Cuoco Pasta con Sarde Seasoning for Macaroni with Sardines
1 lb. pasta of your choice
Grated Pecorino Romano Cheese

Directions:

Measure olive oil into a medium sauce pan. Mince garlic and add to olive oil. Sauté on medium heat until it is light golden brown, stirring so it doesn't burn.

Add tomato paste and water. Stir until well blended. Add tomato sauce and stir, then stir in baking soda and sugar. If it tastes bitter, add additional baking soda 1/8 teaspoon at a time and sugar 1/2 teaspoon at a time.

Cover the pan with a small opening for steam to escape. Cook until it just starts to boil then turn the heat down to low and simmer for 15 minutes stirring after 10 minutes so it doesn't stick to the bottom of the pan and burn.

***Different brands of tomato pastes and tomato sauces have different flavors. If it tastes bitter, you can add additional baking soda and sugar. Add baking soda 1/8 teaspoon at a time and additional sugar ½ teaspoon at a time. Stir and then taste it to see if it is the flavor you like.

Add the can of Pasta con Sarde blend. If the sardines are in large chunks, break them into smaller pieces. Stir well. Simmer on low heat for 15 minutes.

Cook pasta according to package directions. When it is cooked, drain it and return it to the pan. Add a little sauce to the pasta and stir it in so the pasta doesn't stick together.

Serve in individual dishes and then ladle additional Pasta con Sarde sauce on it. Sprinkle with Pecorino Romano cheese.

Serve with a salad and a loaf of your favorite bread!

All Pastas Are Not the Same

Most people think that all pastas are the same, but the varieties are endless. Some are used in specialty recipes, like lasagna or stuffed shells. Some pastas are shaped to hold sauce and larger sizes hold more sauce.

Some common long noodles include spaghetti, angel hair, linguini, and fettuccini, and they come in nests or lengths. Other common pastas include Spirals, Shells, Rigatoni, Cavatelli, Elbows, Ziti, Penne, and Ditali. Others are Tagliatelle, Mostaccioli, Mezze Penne, Penne Rigate, Farfalle, Fiori, Radiatori, Acini di pepe, and Pastina.

The ingredients, shape, texture, and size of pasta used in different recipes influences the taste of these dishes. Ravioli and Tortellini are pastas made with ricotta in addition to flour, salt, and water. Cannelloni and Manicotti can be filled. Some pastas are egg-free or gluten-free.

In a specialty market, you will find many more pastas, some imported. Some of the unique pastas you might find are Vesuviotti, Cavatappi, Creste Di Gallo, Gemelli Anna, Tubetti, Fusilli Avellinese, and Paccheri Rigate.

Each city in Sicily has different pastas and ways to prepare them, like the unique recipes my family brought with them to America. It is my pleasure to share our delicious recipes with you so they can be enjoyed for a very long time!

Stuffed Artichoke

**Sicilian Stuffed
Green Pepper**

Stuffed "Stuff"

**Sicilian Cauliflower
& Ricotta Boglioloti**

**Sicilian Sausage
Bogliolati**

How To Make...

Stuffed Artichoke

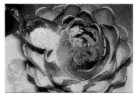

Sicilian Sausage Bogliolati

Sicilian Cauliflower & Ricotta Bogliolati

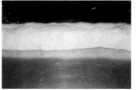 

Stuffed Artichokes

Our family recipe for Stuffed Artichokes has to be the easiest one you will ever find! Give them a try. You won't be disappointed!

Serves 4:

Ingredients:

4 large artichokes
1 (15 oz.) package of Italian Style breadcrumbs
Water + add more if it evaporates while steaming

Directions:

Wash artichokes with water and dry them off. Cut the stems off so they can sit upright in a pan. Use scissors to cut off the sharp tips on each leaf. Hold the artichoke in your hand by the bottom with the top on the counter. Press down on the artichoke so the leaves spread apart to put in the breadcrumb. Put the breadcrumb in a dish. With a spoon, fill each leaf with breadcrumbs. (I put in a lot because I love it!) When they are full, stand them up in a large pan, close together so they don't fall over, and add a half cup of water. (Do not pour it on the artichokes.) Cover the pan and cook on high heat until it starts to boil. Turn down to low and cook for about half an hour. They are ready when you pull on a leaf and it comes off easily.

Eat the stuffed artichokes by scraping the breadcrumb and the soft inside of each leaf with your teeth. When you get to the fuzzy part, remove it and don't eat it. You have now reached the artichoke heart that is soft and scrumptious!

Sicilian Stuffed Green Peppers

Oven 350 degrees
Bake 30 - 45 minutes covered
Bake 15 – 20 minutes uncovered

Ingredients:

3 extra-large green peppers or 5 medium green peppers
1 c. uncooked rice, white or brown
1 T. olive oil
½ large yellow onion, diced
½ lb. lean ground beef
½ lb. ground pork
½ tsp. salt
½ teaspoon black pepper
2 raw eggs
2 tsp. Pecorino Romano cheese
3/4 cup water
Sauce or ketchup (optional)

Directions:

Cook one cup rice following package directions but do not add salt or butter. Set aside when it is cooked.

Sauté the diced onion in olive oil until it is transparent. Add the beef and pork and stir, breaking it into small pieces. Cook until browned. If there is water in the pan after the meat is browned, cook it down until most of the water evaporates. Add the salt and pepper and stir well.

Add 2 ½ cups of the cooked rice to the meat and onion mixture and stir well. Next, stir in the raw eggs and cheese.

Wash and dry the peppers. Cut off the stems. Then cut off the tops and remove the seeds.

Fill a green pepper with the meat/rice mixture, first the bottom and then put some stuffing in the indents in the top of the pepper. Put the top back on the pepper. Spray a casserole pan with non-stick spray and place the pepper in it standing up. Repeat with all of the peppers.

Pour ¾ cup of water in the casserole with the stuffed peppers. Place the cover on the casserole pan and bake for half an hour, then check to see if the water has evaporated. If it has, add ¼ cup more water. Bake covered for another 15 minutes. Remove cover and bake for fifteen to twenty minutes for tops of peppers to brown.

Serve with sauce or ketchup. (optional)

***These freeze well in freezer storage bags/containers. Freeze individually for single-servings. Warm them up in microwave oven.

Being Sicilian, my mother put cheese in everything! She even put it in Polish Pigs in the Blanket. She always said, "You have to put in cheese. You have to have some flavor!" I still laugh every time I think of her saying that. It's like she is standing right next to me.

Sicilian Cauliflower & Ricotta Bogliolati

(Pronounced "Boo You La Tea")

Preheat oven to 350 degrees
Makes 6
Cover baking sheet with parchment paper

Ingredients:

1 ½ lb. pizza dough
1 small head cauliflower cut into bite size pieces
1 c. Ricotta Cheese, whole milk or part skim
¼ tsp. salt
1/8 tsp. pepper
¾ c. shredded mozzarella cheese
2 T. Pecorino Romano cheese
1/2 c. olive oil

Directions:

Lightly flour a 10" x 14" baking sheet and spread dough to fit it edge to edge. Let rise while getting other ingredients ready.

Put cauliflower in a pan and cover with water. Cover pan and bring to a slow boil. Cook on medium heat until it is soft but still firm. Measure 1 1/4 cup. Drain cauliflower in a strainer. Press down gently with the back of a spoon to squeeze water out of it. Put Ricotta Cheese in a strainer and press down on it with a spoon until most of the water is out of it.

54

Spread ricotta over pizza dough leaving a half inch edge of dough. Spread the cauliflower over the ricotta layer. Spread the Mozzarella cheese over the cauliflower and ricotta layer. Sprinkle with Pecorino Romano Cheese.

Lengthwise, roll the dough around all of the ingredients and make sure the edge is well sealed. Pinch the seam together. Cut the roll into 3 inch pieces.

Hold each three-inch piece with an open side down and press some of the side dough to cover the bottom. Leave the top open. Set on the baking sheet.

Brush with olive oil. Bake for 15 minutes. Brush with olive oil again. Turn the baking sheet 180 degrees and bake for another 15 minutes.

Bake until they are golden brown. If they are brown but don't seem fully cooked, you can cover them with aluminum foil and bake for another 10 minutes.

Freeze individually in baggies. Warm in a microwave oven on low for about 2 – 3 minutes and serve.

Sicilian Sausage Bogliolati

Preheat oven to 350 degrees
Makes 6
Cover baking sheet with parchment paper

Ingredients:

1 1/2 lb. pizza dough
1 1/4 lb. hot or sweet Italian Sausage; pork, chicken or turkey sausage
¼ c. water
1 1/4 c. shredded mozzarella cheese; whole milk or part skim milk
1/3 c. grated Pecorino Romano cheese
Olive oil

Directions:

Lightly flour a 10" x 14" baking sheet and spread dough to fit it edge to edge. Let rise while getting other ingredients ready.

Remove sausage from casings and break into bite-size pieces. Brown in ¼ cup water and cook until water is evaporated. If there is water left when the sausage is browned, remove it with a spoon. If you use pork sausage and it is greasy, remove the grease from it before spreading it on the dough.

Spread the cooked sausage over the dough leaving a half inch edge of dough. Press in lightly. Spread shredded mozzarella cheese over the sausage. Sprinkle with Pecorino Romano Cheese.

Lengthwise, roll the dough around all of the ingredients and pinch the seam together so it is well sealed. Twist the roll from one end to the other. It will become a little longer when you do this so you will get more boglioloti. Slice into approximately 4 inch pieces.

Form each slice into round shape with open edges slightly folded toward the center of the filled area and place on baking sheet with open ends on the bottom and top. Repeat with all cut pieces.

Brush each with olive oil. Bake for 15 minutes. Turn the pan and brush with oil again and bake for another 15 minutes until they are golden brown. You can cover lightly with a piece of aluminum foil and bake for another 10 or so minutes to make sure they are well cooked inside.

Freeze individually in baggies. Warm in a microwave oven on low for about 2 – 3 minutes and serve.

Notes

Sicilian Sausage Pizza

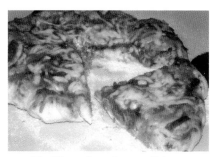
Sicilian Anchovy Pizza

Main Dish Pizza

Sicilian Covered Pizza

How To Make...

Sicilian Anchovy Pizza

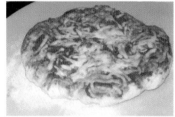

Sicilian Covered Pizza

Pizza Dough

Use this easy home-made dough for pizza or Bogliolati. It is a very economical way to make your favorite dishes, another "Cucina Povera" recipe! Mix with an electric mixer using the dough hook or you can mix it by hand.

For pizza, pre-heat oven to 400 degrees
Bake 20 minutes
Enough for 1 pizza or one recipe of bogliolati

Ingredients:

2 ½ c. all-purpose flour
1 envelope yeast
¼ tsp. salt
1 ¼ c. warm water

Note: Use a yeast that you can add to your dry ingredients, one that does not have to be dissolved in liquid before adding to flour. Dr. Oetker brand is one such yeast.

Toppings for Sausage Pizza:

½ lb. hot or mild Italian sausage
15 oz. can or jar of pizza sauce
4 – 6 oz. shredded Mozzarella cheese
2 T. grated Pecorino Romano cheese
Add additional toppings of your choice

Directions:

Place 2 ½ cups of flour in a large mixing bowl and stir in the package of yeast and the salt. Pour in one cup of the water and mix with the electric mixer on slow. Add the rest of the water and continue mixing until a soft dough is formed. Place some flour on a board and knead the dough until it is smooth and elastic. Add enough flour so the dough isn't sticky. (You might use half to one cup of additional flour.)

Sprinkle flour in a warm bowl and put the dough in it. Cover it and place in a warm spot away from drafts. Let it rise for about an hour and a half, until it doubles in bulk.

Stretch the dough to fit a 10" pizza pan that has been sprayed with non-stick spray or on a pizza stone which has been sprinkled with corn meal. Cover it and let it rise again.

Add toppings:

Break sausage into bite size pieces and brown lightly in a frying pan. Spread the sausage on the pizza dough, pressing it into the dough a little. Spread the sauce over the sausage. Next, spread the shredded mozzarella cheese and top off with the Pecorino Romano cheese.

Bake until the pizza is golden brown and the fillings are hot and bubbly. Let sit for 5 minutes before serving.

"My mother, Lucia, always made her pizza in a 10" x 15" baking sheet. You can do that if you like."

Sicilian Anchovy Pizza

Preheat oven to 350 degrees
Bake 18 - 20 minutes
Serves 2

Ingredients:

½ lb. pizza dough
1 (2 oz.) tin flat anchovies cut into small pieces
1 T. finely chopped fresh garlic
¼ c. tomato sauce
½ c. shredded mozzarella cheese
Cornmeal spread on a pizza stone or
non-stick cooking spray on a pizza pan

Directions:

Spread the pizza dough into an 8-inch circle on a pizza pan
or pizza stone. Put pieces of anchovies on the top of the
pizza dough pressing them in slightly. Spread the chopped
garlic on next. Spread the sauce on the pizza. Lastly,
spread the cheese on top of the other toppings.

Bake at 350 degrees for 15 minutes. Pizza should be
slightly browned on top. Remove from oven when done
and let it rest for five minutes. Cut into two pieces. Serve.

To make a 12-inch pizza, use 1 pound of pizza dough,
double all toppings and follow directions for the 8-inch
pizza. Bake for 20 minutes and check for doneness. Edges
should be browned and puffy. When done, remove from
oven and let it rest for 5 minutes before serving. Cut pizza
in 4 – 6 pieces. Serve.

Sicilian Covered Pizza

On Christmas Eve, Sicilians do not eat meat but the meals we had were decadent. We enjoyed foods reserved for that once-a-year dinner. We started with salad, followed by Sicilian Covered Pizza, filled with potatoes and onions. The meal also included octopus, fried cod, snails, and tomato and cheese pizza, all home made by my mother and father.

For dessert, we had Sicilian Ribbon Cookies, Cannoli, Cream Puffs, and a selection of Christmas cookies. My aunt Frances always made a Cassata, a special Christmas cake made of sponge cake, ricotta cream, almonds, milk chocolate, candied fruit, and maraschino cherries. The holidays were a very special time with special foods prepared for family and friends.

Preheat oven 375 degrees
Bake 35 minutes
Spray baking sheet with non-stick spray

Ingredients:

3 lb. pizza dough, home-made or store bought
2 T. olive oil
2 c. sliced yellow onions
3 ½ lb. white potatoes
¾ tsp. salt
¼ tsp. pepper
1 T. olive oil to brush top of pizza

Directions:

Make or buy pizza dough. Divide the dough into two one-and-a-half pound balls. Cover a large cookie sheet with parchment paper. Spray with non-stick spray. Place the pizza dough balls on the parchment paper leaving space between them. Preheat the oven to 200 degrees and then turn it off. Place the cookie sheet with the dough on it in the oven on the middle rack. Let it rise until it doubles in size.

Peel and slice onions. Peel and cut potatoes into bite size pieces. Put 2 tablespoons olive oil in a large frying pan, add the potatoes and then the onions. Stir them together. Add salt and pepper and stir. Turn heat to low, cover pan and cook 5 to 7 minutes. Take off the cover and continue to cook until the potatoes are tender, stirring gently so they don't stick to the bottom of the pan.

Press one ball of pizza dough on a baking sheet covered with parchment paper and sprayed with non-stick cooking spray. Spread it out to a 14" x 10" rectangle. Put the rolled out dough into the oven to rise for about 20 minutes.

Spread the potato and onion mixture evenly on the dough leaving a couple inches around the edge. Press the second piece of dough into a 14" x 10" rectangle and place on top of the potato and onions. Fold the edge of the bottom piece of dough over the top piece and seal the edges well.

Sprinkle 1 tablespoon of olive oil on the top of the pizza and press gently with your fingertips all over it so the oil goes into the small indentations you make.

Bake for 35 minutes or until golden brown. Let it set for about 10 minutes before cutting and serving.

Notes

Sicilian Ribbon Cookies

Sweet Ravioli

Honey Drizzled Pastries

Cavatelli

How To Make...

Sicilian Ribbon Cookies

Sweet Ravioli

Cavatelli

Sicilian Ribbon Cookies

One of the special desserts my mother made for Christmas each year was Sicilian Ribbon Cookies. We waited all year for the ribbons and knots of these sweet cookies drizzled with honey and sprinkled with confectionery sugar.

Before the holiday, my mother baked endlessly to prepare all the wonderful desserts and pastries for family and friends who dropped by during the holidays. My father helped her by deep-frying the ribbons to a light golden brown while my mother cut the strips and tied them into knots and bows.

After they were deep-fried, they were stored in a large old-fashioned laundry basket filled to the top!

When people stopped by, my mother would "fix" a dish of ribbons, drizzling them with honey and sprinkling them with confectionery sugar. When you bit into them, they were a surprise of a light pastry and the sweetness of honey!

"When my mother, Lucia, was in high school, her father needed her help on the farm and was going to make her quit school. The principal from her school went to the farm to talk to her father, asking him if mom could stay in school. He would arrange her studies so she could get her high school diploma in three years. Her father agreed to let her finish school and she received her high school diploma on June 28, 1938."

Sicilian Ribbon Cookies

Ingredients:

1 lb. flour
1 ½ tsp. baking powder
¼ c. sugar
1 ½ tsp. Crisco
6 eggs, beaten
½ tsp. vanilla
1 ½ tsp. whiskey

3 – 4 c. Crisco to deep fry ribbons
Honey
Confectionery sugar

Directions:

Weigh the flour and put it into a large bowl. Stir in the baking powder and sugar. Add the 1 ½ teaspoon Crisco to the flour mixture and break it up in the flour with a fork. Set aside until egg mixture is ready.

In a large mixing bowl, with electric mixer, beat the eggs well. Add the vanilla and whiskey to the eggs and beat again. Pour about 1/3 of the flour mixture into the egg mixture and mix with electric mixer. Add another third of the flour but stir it in as the dough will get thicker. Add the last third of the flour and mix it by hand. If it is still sticky, add a little more flour. Put some flour on a dough board or counter and knead the dough until it forms a smooth ball.

Divide the dough into 6 smaller balls. Sprinkle some flour on the counter where you are going to roll out the dough. Put a ball of dough on the flour, flatten it out with your hand, and sprinkle flour on top of it so it doesn't stick to the rolling pin. Roll the dough out very thin, 14 inches long and 10 inches wide. Cut ½ inch wide strips using a wheel cutter or knife and tie each strip in a knot or bow.

Measure 3 to 4 cups of Crisco into a medium saucepan. Warm on low temperature until the Crisco is melted. Heat the Crisco on medium to high heat and bring to a boil. Put in one of the ribbons. It if floats right away, the oil is hot enough to cook the bows.

Gently drop one or two ribbons at a time into the hot oil. They will float. Push them down gently, but just for a few seconds as they can easily burn, then turn the bows over. Take them out of the oil as soon as they are light golden brown. Place on a wire rack so any oil drains off of them.

Store uncovered in a cool dry place.

Directions to "fix" ribbon cookies to serve:

Lay the ribbon cookies on a serving platter in one layer. Drizzle this layer of ribbon cookies with honey. Add another layer and drizzle with honey. You can add a third layer of ribbons and drizzle with honey. Put confectionery sugar in a small strainer and sprinkle the top layer.

Sweet Ravioli

Makes about 24
Serve 4 – 5 per person

Ingredients:

Dough:

1 ¾ c. flour
1 ½ T. butter
1 ½ T. Crisco
Water

2 – 3 c. Crisco to deep fry
Honey and confectionery
sugar to "fix"

Filling:

1 c. Ricotta Cheese
1 whole egg
1 egg yolk
2 T. sugar
½ tsp. vanilla

Directions:

Dough:

In a bowl, mix flour, butter and Crisco with a pastry blender. Add 2 tablespoons water and mix well. Add more water one tablespoon at a time and mix. Add water until the dough can be formed into a smooth ball. Divide it into two parts.

Filling:

Combine the ricotta cheese, whole egg, egg yolk, sugar and vanilla and stir until smooth.

To make ravioli:

Roll half of the dough into a 12" x 12" square. Trim edges so they are all straight. Cut it lengthwise into 3 four-inch wide strips. Separate the strips so they are easier to work with.

Place four separate teaspoons of filling lengthwise down the right side of the dough equally separated. Fold the left side of the dough over the right side of the dough over the filling. Seal the long edge and both ends by pressing down with the tines of a fork. Press between each filled section and cut apart. Seal each cut side with the tines of fork. Repeat this with the other two strips from this half of the dough. Repeat with the other half of the dough. If you have extra pieces of dough, make a ball, roll it out, and make more sweet ravioli or cut them into strips and deep fry.

To deep fry:

Heat 2 – 3 cups of Crisco in a medium sized pan on high. When it is hot, carefully drop two of the ravioli into the Crisco. With tongs, gently press them down into the hot oil. Check to make sure they don't burn. When bottom sides are golden brown, turn over. When they are golden brown on both sides, take them out and stand them upright on a cooling rack so oil will drip off of them. Repeat with all of the ravioli.

To "fix":

Arrange the amount you want to serve on a plate and drizzle with honey. Sprinkle with confectionery sugar using a small mesh strainer. Refrigerate the rest of the fried sweet ravioli in a sealed container. When you want to serve them, "fix" them on a plate with honey.

Cavatelli

Cavatelli are delicious and unique Christmas cookies that are sweetened with honey and sugar. They are one of my favorites! I can't wait to have them only for Christmas so I make them throughout the year. I put them in the freezer in baggies, without the honey on them, and grab a few out to eat whenever I have a craving for them!

Pre-heat oven to 375 degrees
Cover cookie sheets with parchment paper
Makes about 14 cups of cookies

Ingredients:

Cookie dough

1 ½ c. sugar
Warm water
2 lb. box of cake flour
2 tsp. baking powder
2 beaten eggs
1 tsp. vanilla
1 ½ c. Crisco
Flour for dipping fork/knife

To "fix" the cookies

½ c. honey
2 tsp. sugar
1/8 tsp. cinnamon
2 shakes cloves (optional)
3 c. baked cavatelli
8 oz. whole raw almonds, cut and toasted
Non-pareil sprinkles

Directions to make cookies:

Measure sugar in a two cup measuring cup. Add water to the same level as the sugar to dissolve the sugar. Stir. Set aside.

Add the baking powder to the cake flour, right in the flour box, and stir it in. Set aside.

Beat the eggs in a separate bowl. Add the vanilla. Set aside.

With an electric mixer cream the Crisco using the regular beater. Add the sugar and water mixture. Continue to mix until blended. Add the beaten eggs and continue to mix.

Add the flour, a little at a time, to the liquid ingredients. Beat in-between additions of the flour. At this point, change to the bread dough hook. Finish by kneading dough by hand so it is soft and smooth. Divide dough into 3 pieces and form each into a smooth ball. Cover these with plastic wrap so they don't get dry while you are forming the cavatelli.

Put 1/2 cup of flour into a drinking glass to dip knife and fork into while forming cookies.

Start with one ball of dough. Break off a piece that can fit in the palm of your hand and return the rest of it to under the plastic wrap. Roll the piece of dough into a roll 1-foot-long and ½ an inch round. Add a little flour so it doesn't stick to the counter top. Cut the roll into ¾ inch pieces. Dip the knife in flour before cutting so the dough doesn't stick to the knife.

To form each piece of dough, dip fork in flour. Place a piece of the dough on the top of the fork tine and press down with your thumb. Roll the piece of dough downward and off the fork so it gets the impression from the fork tines and curls. Place individual cookies half an inch apart in rows on a cookie sheet with the open curled side down. Repeat this with all of the ¾ inch pieces of dough. Then form the next length of dough from the first ball of dough. Continue until the cookie sheet is full.

Bake for about 8 minutes. Stir them on the cookie sheet. Bake another 6 minutes until lightly brown. The longer you bake them, the darker and crunchier they will be.

Remove from the oven. Let sit for a couple minutes on the baking sheet and then put them on a cooling rack.

Repeat this until all the dough has been made into small cookies, baked and cooled. Store in zip lock bags until ready to fix or freeze in freezer bags for later use.

Directions to toast the almonds:

Cut each raw almond into four pieces and place on a cookie sheet that has low sides. Bake in a pre-heated 375 degree oven for about 2 – 3 minutes then stir every 30 seconds while they continue to bake until they are toasted. The longer you toast them, the crunchier they will be. Check them often as they burn easily.

Directions to fix the cookies to serve:

In a small sauce pan, on low heat, warm the honey with the sugar. Add the cinnamon and cloves. Put in the cookies and toasted almonds. Fold very gently with a wooden spoon so all the cookies and almonds are coated with honey. Put cookies on a plate and sprinkle with the nonpareils. Serve.

Cannoli

Cream Puffs

Cake, Cream Puffs & Cannoli

Cassata

How To Make...

Cannoli Shells

Cream Puffs Shells

Cannoli Shells

Cannoli with Ricotta Cream or Sicilian Cream are a pastry that we only enjoyed for Christmas. My mother would make the dough, cut the shapes, put them on the canes, and my father would deep fry them. This recipe makes about fourteen cannoli shells but my mother would make many more because we had a lot of family and friends for the holidays. The recipe she made in 1968 called for ten cups of flour. It made approximately forty-five shells. It took about three or four recipes of the creams to fill them.

Before you make the cannoli, make a holder out of a wire hanger to hold the cane with the cannoli on it while you cook it. See the photo of the holder. You can buy the metal "canes" at a specialty kitchen store.

Makes about 14 cannoli shells

Ingredients:

3 1/3 c. cake flour
1 egg yolk
Crisco, the size of a walnut
1/3 c. sugar (dissolved in hot wine)
1 c. of burgundy wine, plus a little more if needed
1 egg white, beaten
Flour or cake flour, enough to roll out the dough
5 – 6 c. Crisco for deep frying

Sicilian Cream or Ricotta Cream to fill Cannoli (2 recipes)
Milk chocolate candy bar
6 oz. raw sliced almonds, cut into smaller pieces, toasted

Directions:

Separate the egg and save the white in a small bowl. Mix the egg yolk and Crisco with the flour in a large bowl. Measure sugar in a measuring cup and add burgundy wine to cover the sugar. Heat in microwave for about 40 seconds to heat the wine so the sugar dissolves. Pour wine/sugar mixture into the flour and mix well. Add more wine, about a quarter cup at a time, and mix. Add more wine as needed until you can form the dough into a ball. Divide dough into three smaller balls of dough.

Sprinkle some flour on counter and place one ball of dough in the middle. Sprinkle some flour on the top. Start rolling from the middle outward in all directions. Pick up the dough with the rolling pin. Add more flour to the counter and put down the dough. Sprinkle flour on top. Continue rolling out the dough until it is thin. Cut oval shapes around a saucer. Wrap them on the canes, brush a little of the egg white on the edge of the dough and press the seam to seal.

Heat five cups Crisco in a heavy pan until it starts to bubble. Put a small flat piece of the dough in the pan to see if the Crisco is hot enough. The dough should float quickly. When the Crisco is hot enough, hold a cannoli on the cane with the holder so it is covered with the hot oil. Hold the cannoli in the Crisco turning it so it browns on all sides. Take out and place on a cooling rack. Deep fry all of the cannoli. Remove the canes. Store in a cool dry place covered loosely with paper towels.

Toast almonds. Break raw sliced almonds into smaller pieces. Spread them out on a cookie sheet. Toast in oven set at 350 degrees for about 4 minutes. Stir them. Keep an eye on them so they don't burn. Keep toasting for about three to four minutes at a time, checking and turning them, until they are a light golden brown. Cool completely. Store in a sealed container.

Make two recipes of Ricotta Cream or Sicilian Cream to fill all of the cannoli. Cool in refrigerator. Cut small pieces of milk chocolate and stir in the cream. Add as much or as little chocolate as you like. Fill cannoli with cream. Dip ends in toasted almonds and sprinkle with confectionery sugar.

Fill cannoli right before serving so the shells don't get soggy. Cover and refrigerate any filled cannoli.

***If you do not want to make your own cannoli shells, you can buy pre-made shells at specialty Italian markets; but home-made are definitely better!

Cream Puff Shells

Ingredients:

1 c. all-purpose flour
1 T. sugar
1/8 tsp. salt
1 c. water
1/3 c. butter
4 eggs at room temperature
Confectionery sugar

Directions:

A couple hours before you plan to make creampuffs, take the eggs out of the refrigerator. They need to be at room temperature for the dough to puff when baked.

Combine flour, sugar and salt in a bowl, stir and set aside.

In a heavy pan combine water and butter and bring to a boil. When the butter is melted, drop the flour mixture into the water all at one time and stir quickly with a wooden spoon. It will start to become smooth and that is when you stir faster until the dough does not stick to the sides of the pan. As soon as it is no longer shiny, remove pan from the stove.

Add eggs one at a time beating well with an electric mixer. The dough will look lumpy and shiny. When it gets sticky and the shine is almost gone, add another egg and beat. Continue with each egg until you have added all of the eggs. The dough will stick together and not be shiny when it is ready to use. Use the dough right away.

Place a tablespoon full of dough in a smooth round heap on the baking sheet. Put a teaspoon more of dough on the top of the first heap, smoothing it. Place heaps of dough 2 – 3 inches apart. Continue until you have used all the dough.

When they are all on the baking sheet, with water on your finger, smooth all of them. Gently sprinkle a little water onto the baking sheet with your fingers as if you are sprinkling clothes to iron.

Bake the creampuffs at 400 degrees for 10 minutes and then reduce temperature to 350 degrees and bake for another 25 minutes. Make sure puffs are firm to the touch before removing them from the oven. Be careful to not leave them in too long as you don't want them to burn. Remove from the oven and leave on baking sheet for 5 minutes. Transfer them to a cooling rack and cool them completely before filling.

After they have cooled, with a sharp knife, cut each puff horizontally where the bottom part meets the top part. Take out any raw puff dough that remains inside.

Fill the bottom and the top with Sicilian Cream or Ricotta Cream and put the top back on. Put them on a serving plate. Sprinkle with confectionary sugar using a small mesh strainer and serve.

Sicilian Cream

This Sicilian Cream recipe came from my great-aunt, Mariassunta, who came from Siculiana, Sicily. Besides creampuffs, we also use this cream to fill cannoli and mix it with cooked wheat to enjoy for The Feast of Saint Lucy.

Ingredients:

1/3 c. plus 2 T. all-purpose flour
½ c. sugar
¼ tsp. salt
2 c. hot milk
1 egg slightly beaten
1 T. butter
1 tsp. vanilla flavoring

Directions:

Measure flour, sugar and salt into a heavy sauce pan. While milk is still cold, pour about 1/3 cup of it into the pan and mix with a wire whisk until it is smooth and creamy. If it is too thick to mix, add a little more milk and whisk again. Bring the rest of the milk to a boil in the microwave and then pour into the creamy mixture in the pan. Whisk it together.

Cook on medium heat, whisking continuously, until the mixture thickens. Remove from the heat and add the butter and the beaten egg, stirring so the egg doesn't cook. Return to heat for about 2 minutes stirring constantly. Remove from heat and stir in the vanilla. Cool the cream in refrigerator before filling creampuffs.

Ricotta Cream

Sicilian Ricotta Cream recipe that we use for Sicilian Cassata and to fill cannoli and cream puffs.

Ingredients:

½ c. cornstarch
2/3 c. sugar
2 c. milk
1 ¼ lb. ricotta cheese (about 2 cups)
½ tsp. vanilla
½ tsp. lemon extract

Directions:

Whisk together cornstarch and sugar in a heavy saucepan. Slowly whisk in ½ to ¾ cup of the milk until it is combined and smooth. Whisk in the remainder of the milk. Cook on medium heat stirring continuously with a whisk until it thickens. Add the ricotta to the mixture. Continue to cook, stirring, for about five minutes until it is combined and smooth. Stir in the vanilla flavoring and lemon extract. Put in a bowl, cover and refrigerate. Cool completely before assembling cassata, or filling cannoli or cream puffs. Stir Ricotta Cream before using it on the cake or in cannoli or cream puffs.

Sponge Cake for Sicilian Cassata

Makes 2 (8 or 9 inch) layers
Preheat oven 350 degrees
Prepare cake pans (see "To bake," below)
Bake 40 to 50 minutes

Ingredients:

1 ¼ c. cake flour
½ tsp. baking powder
1 c. sugar
½ tsp. salt

6 egg yolks
½ c. sugar
¼ c. cold water

¾ tsp. vanilla flavoring
¾ tsp. lemon extract

6 egg whites
1 tsp. cream of tartar

Directions:

In a bowl combine cake flour, baking powder, 1 cup sugar, and salt. Set aside.

In a mixing bowl, beat the egg yolks with an electric mixer. Gradually add ½ cup sugar and ¼ c. water while continuing to beat until it is smooth. Add the vanilla flavoring and lemon extract. Continue to beat.

Add the flour mixture to the egg yolk mixture and beat well. Set aside. In a separate mixing bowl, with an electric mixer, beat the egg whites with the cream of tartar until stiff peaks form. Pour the egg yolk mixture into the stiff egg whites. With a spatula or wooden spoon, gently fold the egg yolk mixture into the stiff egg whites until well blended.

To bake:

Grease the bottoms and sides of 2 8" or 9" inch spring form pans or cake pans with Crisco. Dust with all-purpose flour. Set the baking pans on wax paper and trace around them. Cut out the circles and place on the inside bottoms of the pans. Grease and flour wax paper.

Pour equal amounts of cake batter into baking pans and make sure batter is level. Bake on middle rack of oven for 40 minutes. Check for doneness by lightly pressing your finger into the top of the cake. If the cake springs back when you lift your finger, it is done. If not, let it bake another 10 minutes. Tops should be lightly browned. Again, check for doneness. When done, remove from oven.

Let the cakes cool for 15 minutes in the pans. Run a butter knife around the edge of the cakes to release them. If you use spring form pans, undo the sides and remove from both cakes. If you used regular cake pans, turn the cakes upside down to remove from the pans. Peel off wax paper. Lay cakes on cooling racks with bottom sides down. Let cool completely.

Sicilian Cassata: How To Assemble

What you need:

2 layers sponge cake (Recipe on page 80)
1 recipe Ricotta Cream (Recipe on page 79)
1 T. candied fruit cake mix
Milk chocolate cut into small pieces
Maraschino cherries drained well and cut in half
Toasted slivered almonds

Directions:

Preheat oven to 350 degrees. Put almonds on a baking sheet with sides. Toast in oven for about five minutes. Stir often so they don't burn. Cool before putting on the cake.

Place one layer of cake, rounded side down, on a plate. Cover top and side with ricotta cream. Put candied fruit cake mix and chocolate pieces sparingly on top of the frosted cake layer. Place second cake layer with rounded side up on frosted bottom layer. Cover top and side of this layer with cream. Smooth cream over the entire cake. Cut the maraschino cherries in half. Place maraschino cherries, rounded side up, around the edge of the top of the cake about 1/4 inch from the edge. Cover the side of the cake with toasted almonds and the top with pieces of chocolate.

Refrigerate Cassata for 2 hours before serving. Cover and refrigerate leftover cake.

Saint Lucy's Wheat

Grandma Ruta's Ricotta Pastry

Specialty Cookies, Pastries & Wheat

Bones of the Dead

Soft Molasses Cookies

How To Make...

Grandma Ruta's Ricotta Pastry

Bones of the Dead

Saint Lucy's Wheat

Ingredients:

1 lb. peeled wheat grain
Water
1 ½ c. Sicilian Cream or Ricotta Cream
Sugar & Cinnamon

Directions:

Put wheat in a large pan. Cover with hot water. Clean the wheat by removing anything that floats. Drain the water out of the pan leaving the wheat in the pan. Repeat this 3 times.

Cover the wheat with hot water. Let it soak for 4 to 5 hours then rinse it one last time. Cover the wheat with hot water at least 2 inches above the top of the wheat. Bring to a boil. Cover the pan with cover tilted so steam can escape. Cook on low for approximately 1½ hours or until wheat is soft when you taste it. If it is not soft enough and the water has been absorbed, add an additional cup of water. You might have to do this more than once. If it seems cooked enough and there is still some water in it, take the cover off and let it cook until most of the water evaporates. Let it cool in the pan for half an hour. Put it into a bowl, cover and refrigerate.

How to "fix" and serve:

Mix 2 cups of cold cooked wheat with 1 ½ cup of cold Sicilian Cream. Sprinkle with cinnamon. Or, serve cold or warm with sugar and cinnamon.

Grandma Ruta's Ricotta Pastry

Grandma Ruta made a simple pastry that has a sweet crust and ricotta filling. It is a recipe that comes from a "Cucina Povera" because it is made with inexpensive ingredients. It is very economical to make so she made enough for everyone who went to the farm on Sunday.

Makes 1 8" pastry
Preheat oven at 375 degrees
Bake 15 minutes
Line a baking pan with parchment paper

Ingredients:

Pastry crust:

1 c. flour
1 tsp. baking powder
1/8 tsp. salt
2 T. + 2 tsp. sugar
1 T. butter
1 egg
Fruit juice or orange juice

Ricotta Filling:

½ c. ricotta cheese
1 egg
1 T. sugar
Dash of cinnamon

Directions:

For pastry crust:

Combine the flour, baking powder, salt, sugar and butter. Mix until the butter is incorporated into the flour mixture.

Put in the egg and mix. It will be dry and lumpy. Add orange juice a tablespoon at a time and mix until the dough is soft but not sticky. If you put in too much juice, add a little flour. Form it into a smooth ball.

Line a cookie sheet with parchment paper. Spray with non-stick cooking spray. Put the ball of dough in the middle of the cookie sheet and press the dough into an 8 inch round pastry crust with a raised edge; about ¾ inch high so the filling with stay in it. Flute the edge.

For filling:

Put all of the filling ingredients in a two cup measuring cup. Stir until it is well blended. Pour the filling into the crust and smooth the top evenly. Bake for 12 minutes and then check to see if it is done. The ricotta should look firm and dry and the crust light golden brown. When you lightly touch the top with your fingertip, the ricotta filling should not come off onto your finger.

Cool for about 15 minutes. This recipe makes 4 servings. Cover and refrigerate.

To double this recipe:

Makes 1 11" pastry
8 servings

Double all ingredients for the pastry crust and double the ingredients for the ricotta filling. Follow the directions for the 8-inch pastry but press the dough into an 11 inch round pastry crust.

Bones of the Dead

This recipe for Sicilian Bones of the Dead, or Ossa di Morte, shows how unique the recipes are that have been passed down in my family, this recipe coming from Pozzalo, Sicily. Our recipes are unique but this recipe might strike you as being a little strange because of its name.

Preheat oven 375 degrees
Makes 6 dozen
Line cookie sheet with parchment paper

Ingredients:

4 c. confectionery sugar
1 ¼ c. flour
4 tsp. baking powder
1 tsp. cinnamon
4 beaten eggs

Water to add if dough is too dry

Directions:

In a large bowl mix the confectionery sugar, flour, baking powder and cinnamon.

In a separate bowl, with an electric mixer, beat the eggs.

Add the eggs to the flour/sugar mixture and mix with a wooden spoon. Dough will be lumpy and dry until the eggs are mixed in well. Continue to mix in the eggs by hand until it forms a dough that you can work into a ball. If it is sticky, add a little flour and mix it in. If it is too dry, add a teaspoon of water at a time and mix in until you can form the dough into a ball that is firm and not sticky.

Work on a lightly floured surface. Take a handful-size portion of dough and roll into a long, thick rope about a half inch around. Cut diagonally into 3 ½ inch long pieces.

Place 3 ½ inch pieces on the cookie sheet 2 inches apart. Spacing is necessary. Repeat this with all of the cookie dough.

Let stand overnight to dry cookies.

The next day, bake cookies at 375 degrees for 11 minutes or until they are golden brown and crusty/hard. A pool of sugar comes out of the cookies as they bake.

Ossa di Morte are sweet and great for dunking in coffee!

Soft Molasses Cookies

On her recipe card, Mom had written, "(When Single), in the corner. She started making these before she got married, in 1945, so this is a very old, and delicious, recipe.

Preheat oven 375 degrees
Bake 12 minutes
Makes about 6 dozen
Line a baking sheet with parchment paper

Ingredients:

1 c. Crisco
1 c. brown sugar
2 eggs
1 c. molasses
3 tsp. baking soda
1 c. hot water
1 c. chopped walnuts,
chocolate chips, or raisins

5 c. flour
1 tsp. ginger
1 tsp. cinnamon
½ tsp nutmeg
¼ tsp. cloves

Directions:

Measure hot water in a measuring cup, add the baking soda and stir to dissolve. Set aside. In a bowl, combine and mix together the flour, ginger, cinnamon, nutmeg, and cloves. Set aside.

Measure Crisco, brown sugar, eggs, and molasses into a mixing bowl and beat with electric mixer until smooth. Add the water with the baking soda and continue beating. Add a third of the flour mixture and beat. Slowly add the rest and mix well. Stir in walnuts, chocolate chips, and/or raisins.

Drop dough by rounded teaspoons on cookie sheet 3 inches apart. Bake 12 minutes.

Lemon Meringue Pie

Chocolate Pie

Pies, Pies & More Pies

Pam's Peach Pie

Apple Pie

Cherry Pie

How To Make...

Pie Crust & How to Roll It Out

One Crust & How to Make

Two Crust Pies & How to Fill & Cover

127648C-bp-10bk

Picking Raspberries with Mom
...and Pam's Peach Pie!

Picking fruit with mom was something I did throughout my life! We started in June when the strawberries were ripe. Most years we picked about twenty-four quarts, freezing some for the winter and also making jam.

Raspberries were next followed by cherries, peaches, pears, and apricots. We had our own trees in our yard. Lastly, we picked apples at Owen Orchard. Mom canned all of these fruits so we would have them until they were available again the following year. We always had enough!

But back to berries! One summer, I went picking raspberries with Mom! My father had told my mother where to find bushes filled with ripe red raspberries! We went to an overgrown field somewhere in the country where only weeds and scrubby looking trees grew; but there were raspberries! We found some really nice bushes filled with delicious looking red raspberries and we were quickly filling up our bowls. I think we ate as many as we put into our bowls; at least I did! Then my mother went in one direction and I went in the other.

A little later I heard my mother scream! I went running to her afraid that she had gotten hurt. When I reached her, she was sitting on the ground, her bowl in her hands; empty! She had a distressed look on her face; scrunched up forehead, sad eyes, and turned down lips. She was on the verge of tears. Then I heard her say, "My berries!" I asked her where they were. She whined, "In the hole!" (Almost 40 years later I still laugh when I think about this!)

At this point I was thinking that she was nuts, but in front of where she was sitting there was a big hole. She had tripped and fallen when she "found" the hole with one of her feet! Her raspberries were gone! I think some gophers filled their tummies with beautiful ripe red raspberries that day!

Years later when my daughter, Pam, was a little girl, we started picking fruit together just like I did with my mother! Pam went "Picking Berries with Mom," but I was the mom now! She got busy with high school and college. Those were the years I picked alone. When she graduated from college we both lived in Rochester, NY and we started picking fruit together again; raspberries, blackberries, and blueberries. But every year I made Pam one of her favorite fruit pies; peach! I made her one in 2014 when she visited me in Florida where I had lived for 4 ½ years! When I pricked it with a fork so the steam could escape, I pricked it with the letter "P" for peach, then realized that it was the first letter in her name. So I pricked the rest of her name on the pie! I will continue to make a peach pie for Pam whenever we are together, when the peaches are ripe and ready for picking!

Pie Crust & Fillings

***Recipe makes crust for <u>one two-crust pie, on page 94, or two one-crust pies, starting below.</u>**

Raspberry pie? Peach pie? Apple pie? Cherry pie? Chocolate pie? Lemon Meringue Pie? Banana Cream Pie? Choose your favorite!

Pie Crust Recipe

Preheat oven to temperatures listed for different pies.

Ingredients:

3/4 c. Crisco
2 c. all-purpose flour
1 tsp. salt
6 T. cold water

Directions:

Combine flour and salt in a large bowl. Cut in Crisco with a pastry blender until it is uniform and still course. Measure the water and sprinkle on the flour/Crisco mixture one tablespoon at a time. Stir it in with a wooden spoon until it starts to look like a firm dough. Finish mixing it with your hands and form it into a ball.

DIRECTIONS FOR 2 ONE-CRUST PIES:

Divide pie dough into two smooth balls. Wrap one in plastic wrap and set aside while you roll out the other.

Rolling out the pie crust for one crust pies:

Sprinkle flour on the area where you are going to roll out the pie dough. Place dough ball on the flour and sprinkle flour on top of the dough. (I roll my pie dough in a Pie Crust Bag.) Roll out the dough starting from the center going toward the edges. Pick up the dough and turn it 90 degrees. Repeat this, adding a little more flour under the crust and on top of it so it doesn't stick. (Add more to the Pie Crust Bag.)

Continue rolling the pie dough, turning it until you have a circle larger than your pie plate. Gently roll up the pie crust on the rolling pin and unroll it into the pie plate; or flip over the crust in the Pie Crust Bag onto the pie plate. Cut around the edge leaving about a one-inch overlap.

Fold the edge under to double the thickness around the edge. Flute or press the edge down with a fork. Prick the bottom and sides of the crust before baking.

Bake at 425 degrees for 10 to 15 minutes. Cool crust and fill with filling of your choice. Refrigerate pie.

Directions for fillings for 1 crust pies:

Chocolate Pie Filling

Use 2 boxes of chocolate pudding. Make chocolate pudding following directions on the box. Pour it into the pie crust and cool for 10 minutes. Cover with wax paper and refrigerate.

Banana Cream Pie Filling

Use 2 boxes of vanilla pudding. Make vanilla pudding following directions on box. Slice one or two bananas and place on the bottom of the crust. Pour the vanilla pudding on top of the bananas. Cover with wax paper and refrigerate.

Lemon Meringue Pie Filling & Meringue Topping

Use 2 boxes of lemon pudding. Make lemon pudding following directions on the box. Pour pudding into the crust.

Preheat oven 350 degrees

Ingredients for meringue:

4 egg whites
½ tsp. cream of tartar
6 T. sugar

Directions:

Put egg whites in a mixing bowl and whip until frothy. Add the cream of tartar and continue to beat until they stand in peaks. Beat in sugar one tablespoon at a time. Do not overbeat. Spread on the pie and bake 10 – 15 minutes, depending on the thickness of the meringue. Refrigerate.

DIRECTIONS FOR 1 TWO-CRUST FRUIT PIE:

Prepare fruit filling of your choice following the directions below.

Divide the dough into 2 balls, one a little smaller than the other for the top crust. Press each into a smooth ball. Wrap each in plastic wrap while you prepare the fruit for fruit pies. Set aside.

Roll out the bottom crust the same as you roll out a one crust pie crust, page 91 – 92, but leave an inch-and-a-half overlap.

Pour the filling into the crust.

Roll out the top crust, large enough to cover the filling and overlap the bottom crust to the edge. Place the top crust over the filling and trim the crusts ½ - ¾ inch beyond edge of plate. Fold top edge under bottom crust and flute to seal the edges. Prick the top crust to allow for escape of steam.

Bake following the oven temperatures and times listed at the bottom of each fillings' directions. If the edges start to get too dark, form a ring with aluminum foil to cover just the edges of the pie. Do not cover the middle of the pie. You can also use a purchased metal Pie Edge Protector Ring found in most specialty kitchen supply stores.

Raspberry Pie Filling

Ingredients:
4 c. fresh raspberries
2/3 c. water
¾ c. sugar
¼ tsp. salt
6 T. flour

Directions:

Combine half of the berries and the water in a saucepan. Bring to a boil. Combine the sugar, salt and flour and stir into the hot berries and water mixture. Cook over low heat until thickened, all the time stirring gently. Add the rest of the raspberries and fold in gently so the second addition of the raspberries stay whole. Cool while preparing the pie crust.

Roll out pie crust following directions for 2 crust pie. Fill with raspberry filling and put on top crust. Flute edges. Pierce with a fork for escape of steam.

Bake Raspberry Pie at 400 degrees for 30 minutes or until the top crust is light golden brown.

*** Any of the fruit pies can be frozen unbaked. Wrap well. Do not thaw out before baking. They taste as delicious as fresh!

Peach Pie Filling

Ingredients:
1 c. sugar
3 T. flour
1/4 tsp. salt
8 peaches, peeled and sliced

Directions:

Combine dry ingredients in a bowl and set aside.

Peel the peaches, cut in slices, and place in a large bowl. When all the peaches are sliced, add the dry ingredients and stir together gently.

Roll out pie crust following directions for 2 crust pie. Fill with peach filling and put on top crust. Flute edges. Pierce with a fork for escape of steam.

Bake Peach Pie at 450 degrees for 15 minutes. Turn oven temperature to 350 degrees and bake an additional 35 minutes or until the top crust is light golden brown.

*** When you pierce the top of the pie, pierce the first letter of the kind of pie it is. It really helps when you have more than one fruit pie on your table!

Apple Pie Filling

Ingredients:

8 c. sliced apples
3/4 c. sugar
7 T. flour
1 tsp. cinnamon
2 T. butter

***Use a combination of different varieties of apples to make a tasty pie.

Directions:

Combine the dry ingredients in a bowl and set aside.

Peel the apples and cut into slices. Place in a large bowl. Add the dry ingredients and stir in gently.

Roll out pie crust following directions for 2 crust pie. Fill with apple filling, dot with slices of the butter, and put on top crust. Flute edges. Pierce with a fork for escape of steam.

Bake Apple Pie at 400 degrees for 30 to 40 minutes.

Cherry Pie Filling

Ingredients:

2 (15 oz.) cans cherry pie filling

Directions:

Roll out pie crust following directions for 2 crust pie. Fill with cherry pie filling and put on top crust. Flute edges. Pierce with a fork for escape of steam.

Bake Cherry Pie at 400 degrees for 30 to 40 minutes.

*** Half the fun of making fruit pies is picking your own fruit! Different fruits are ready for picking at different times, from early summer to fall, so each time you pick fruit, you can make a different kind of pie. Your family will love you and everybody will get their favorite!

Index of Recipes

PANTRY BASICS

A WELL-STOCKED PANTRY provides all the makings for a good meal. With the right ingredients, you can quickly create a variety of satisfying, delicious meals for family or guests. Keeping these items in stock also means avoiding extra trips to the grocery store, saving you time and money. Although everyone's pantry is different, there are basic items you should always have. Add other items according to your family's needs. For example, while some families consider chips, cereals and snacks as must-haves, others can't be without feta cheese and imported olives. Use these basic pantry suggestions as a handy reference list when creating your grocery list. Don't forget refrigerated items like milk, eggs, cheese and butter.

STAPLES

Baker's chocolate
Baking powder
Baking soda
Barbeque sauce
Bread crumbs (plain or seasoned)
Chocolate chips
Cocoa powder
Cornmeal
Cornstarch
Crackers
Flour
Honey
Ketchup
Lemon juice
Mayonnaise or salad dressing
Non-stick cooking spray
Nuts (almonds, pecans, walnuts)
Oatmeal
Oil (olive, vegetable)
Pancake baking mix
Pancake syrup
Peanut butter
Shortening
Sugar (granulated, brown, powdered)
Vinegar

PACKAGED/CANNED FOODS

Beans (canned, dry)
Broth (beef, chicken)
Cake mixes with frosting
Canned diced tomatoes
Canned fruit
Canned mushrooms
Canned soup
Canned tomato paste & sauce
Canned tuna & chicken
Cereal
Dried soup mix
Gelatin (flavored or plain)
Gravies
Jarred Salsa
Milk (evaporated, sweetened condensed)
Non-fat dry milk
Pastas
Rice (brown, white)
Spaghetti sauce

SPICES/SEASONINGS

Basil
Bay leaves
Black pepper
Bouillon cubes (beef, chicken)
Chives
Chili powder
Cinnamon
Mustard (dried, prepared)
Garlic powder or salt
Ginger
Nutmeg
Onion powder or salt
Oregano
Paprika
Parsley
Rosemary
Sage
Salt
Soy sauce
Tarragon
Thyme
Vanilla
Worcestershire sauce
Yeast

HERBS & SPICES

DRIED VS. FRESH. While dried herbs are convenient, they don't generally have the same purity of flavor as fresh herbs. Ensure dried herbs are still fresh by checking if they are green and not faded. Crush a few leaves to see if the aroma is still strong. Always store them in an air-tight container away from light and heat.

BASIL
Sweet, warm flavor with an aromatic odor. Use whole or ground. Good with lamb, fish, roast, stews, beef, vegetables, dressing and omelets.

BAY LEAVES
Pungent flavor. Use whole leaf but remove before serving. Good in vegetable dishes, seafood, stews and pickles.

CARAWAY
Spicy taste and aromatic smell. Use in cakes, breads, soups, cheese and sauerkraut.

CELERY SEED
Strong taste which resembles the vegetable. Can be used sparingly in pickles and chutney, meat and fish dishes, salads, bread, marinades, dressings and dips.

CHIVES
Sweet, mild flavor like that of onion. Excellent in salads, fish, soups and potatoes.

CILANTRO
Use fresh. Excellent in salads, fish, chicken, rice, beans and Mexican dishes.

CINNAMON
Sweet, pungent flavor. Widely used in many sweet baked goods, chocolate dishes, cheesecakes, pickles, chutneys and hot drinks.

CORIANDER
Mild, sweet, orangy flavor and available whole or ground. Common in curry powders and pickling spice and also used in chutney, meat dishes, casseroles, Greek-style dishes, apple pies and baked goods.

CURRY POWDER
Spices are combined to proper proportions to give a distinct flavor to meat, poultry, fish and vegetables.

DILL
Both seeds and leaves are flavorful. Leaves may be used as a garnish or cooked with fish, soup, dressings, potatoes and beans. Leaves or the whole plant may be used to flavor pickles.

FENNEL
Sweet, hot flavor. Both seeds and leaves are used. Use in small quantities in pies and baked goods. Leaves can be boiled with fish.

HERBS & SPICES

GINGER
A pungent root, this aromatic spice is sold fresh, dried or ground. Use in pickles, preserves, cakes, cookies, soups and meat dishes.

MARJORAM
May be used both dried or green. Use to flavor fish, poultry, omelets, lamb, stew, stuffing and tomato juice.

MINT
Aromatic with a cool flavor. Excellent in beverages, fish, lamb, cheese, soup, peas, carrots and fruit desserts.

NUTMEG
Whole or ground. Used in chicken and cream soups, cheese dishes, fish cakes, and with chicken and veal. Excellent in custards, milk puddings, pies and cakes.

OREGANO
Strong, aromatic odor. Use whole or ground in tomato juice, fish, eggs, pizza, omelets, chili, stew, gravy, poultry and vegetables.

PAPRIKA
A bright red pepper, this spice is used in meat, vegetables and soups or as a garnish for potatoes, salads or eggs.

PARSLEY
Best when used fresh, but can be used dried as a garnish or as a seasoning. Try in fish, omelets, soup, meat, stuffing and mixed greens.

ROSEMARY
Very aromatic. Can be used fresh or dried. Season fish, stuffing, beef, lamb, poultry, onions, eggs, bread and potatoes. Great in dressings.

SAFFRON
Aromatic, slightly bitter taste. Only a pinch needed to flavor and color dishes such as bouillabaisse, chicken soup, rice, paella, fish sauces, buns and cakes. Very expensive, so where a touch of color is needed, use turmeric instead, but the flavor will not be the same.

SAGE
Use fresh or dried. The flowers are sometimes used in salads. May be used in tomato juice, fish, omelets, beef, poultry, stuffing, cheese spreads and breads.

TARRAGON
Leaves have a pungent, hot taste. Use to flavor sauces, salads, fish, poultry, tomatoes, eggs, green beans, carrots and dressings.

THYME
Sprinkle leaves on fish or poultry before broiling or baking. Throw a few sprigs directly on coals shortly before meat is finished grilling.

TURMERIC
Aromatic, slightly bitter flavor. Should be used sparingly in curry powder and relishes and to color cakes and rice dishes.

Use 3 times more fresh herbs if substituting fresh for dried.

BAKING BREADS

HINTS FOR BAKING BREADS

- Kneading dough for 30 seconds after mixing improves the texture of baking powder biscuits.

- Instead of shortening, use cooking or salad oil in waffles and hot cakes.

- When bread is baking, a small dish of water in the oven will help keep the crust from hardening.

- Dip a spoon in hot water to measure shortening, butter, etc., and the fat will slip out more easily.

- Small amounts of leftover corn may be added to pancake batter for variety.

- To make bread crumbs, use the fine cutter of a food grinder and tie a large paper bag over the spout in order to prevent flying crumbs.

- When you are doing any sort of baking, you get better results if you remember to preheat your cookie sheet, muffin tins or cake pans.

3 RULES FOR USE OF LEAVENING AGENTS

1. In simple flour mixtures, use 2 teaspoons baking powder to leaven 1 cup flour. Reduce this amount 1/2 teaspoon for each egg used.

2. To 1 teaspoon soda, use 2 1/4 teaspoons cream of tartar, 2 cups freshly soured milk or 1 cup molasses.

3. To substitute soda and an acid for baking powder, divide the amount of baking powder by 4. Take that as your measure and add acid according to rule 2.

PROPORTIONS OF BAKING POWDER TO FLOUR

biscuits ....to 1 cup flour use 1 1/4 tsp. baking powder
cake with oil ....to 1 cup flour use 1 tsp. baking powder
muffins ....to 1 cup flour use 1 1/2 tsp. baking powder
popovers ....to 1 cup flour use 1 1/4 tsp. baking powder
waffles ....to 1 cup flour use 1 1/4 tsp. baking powder

PROPORTIONS OF LIQUID TO FLOUR

pour batter ....to 1 cup liquid use 1 cup flour
drop batter ....to 1 cup liquid use 2 to 2 1/2 cups flour
soft dough ....to 1 cup liquid use 3 to 3 1/2 cups flour
stiff dough ....to 1 cup liquid use 4 cups flour

TIME & TEMPERATURE CHART

Breads	Minutes	Temperature
biscuits	12 - 15	400° - 450°
cornbread	25 - 30	400° - 425°
gingerbread	40 - 50	350° - 370°
loaf	50 - 60	350° - 400°
nut bread	50 - 75	350°
popovers	30 - 40	425° - 450°
rolls	20 - 30	400° - 450°

BAKING DESSERTS

PERFECT COOKIES

Cookie dough that must be rolled is much easier to handle after it has been refrigerated for 10 to 30 minutes. This keeps the dough from sticking, even though it may be soft. If not done, the soft dough may require more flour and too much flour makes cookies hard and brittle. Place on a floured board only as much dough as can be easily managed. Flour the rolling pin slightly and roll lightly to desired thickness. Cut shapes close together and add trimmings to dough that needs to be rolled. Place pans or sheets in upper third of oven. Watch cookies carefully while baking in order to avoid burned edges. When sprinkling sugar on cookies, try putting it into a salt shaker in order to save time.

PERFECT PIES

• Pie crust will be better and easier to make if all the ingredients are cool.

• The lower crust should be placed in the pan so that it covers the surface smoothly. Air pockets beneath the surface will push the crust out of shape while baking.

• Folding the top crust over the lower crust before crimping will keep juices in the pie.

• When making custard pie, bake at a high temperature for about 10 minutes to prevent a soggy crust. Then finish baking at a low temperature.

• When making cream pie, sprinkle crust with powdered sugar in order to prevent it from becoming soggy.

PERFECT CAKES

• Fill cake pans two-thirds full and spread batter into corners and sides, leaving a slight hollow in the center.

• Cake is done when it shrinks from the sides of the pan or if it springs back when touched lightly with the finger.

• After removing a cake from the oven, place it on a rack for about 5 minutes. Then, the sides should be loosened and the cake turned out on a rack in order to finish cooling.

• Do not frost cakes until thoroughly cool.

• Icing will remain where you put it if you sprinkle cake with powdered sugar first.

TIME & TEMPERATURE CHART

Dessert	Time	Temperature
butter cake, layer	20 - 40 min.	380° - 400°
butter cake, loaf	40 - 60 min.	360° - 400°
cake, angel	50 - 60 min.	300° - 360°
cake, fruit	3 - 4 hrs.	275° - 325°
cake, sponge	40 - 60 min.	300° - 350°
cookies, molasses	18 - 20 min.	350° - 375°
cookies, thin	10 - 12 min.	380° - 390°
cream puffs	45 - 60 min.	300° - 350°
meringue	40 - 60 min.	250° - 300°
pie crust	20 - 40 min.	400° - 500°

VEGETABLES & FRUITS

COOKING TIME TABLE

Vegetable	Cooking Method	Time
artichokes	boiled	40 min.
	steamed	45-60 min.
asparagus tips	boiled	10-15 min.
beans, lima	boiled	20-40 min.
	steamed	60 min.
beans, string	boiled	15-35 min.
	steamed	60 min.
beets, old	boiled or steamed	1-2 hours.
beets, young with skin	boiled	30 min.
	steamed	60 min.
	baked	70-90 min.
broccoli, flowerets	boiled	5-10 min.
broccoli, stems	boiled	20-30 min.
brussels sprouts	boiled	20-30 min.
cabbage, chopped	boiled	10-20 min.
	steamed	25 min.
carrots, cut across	boiled	8-10 min.
	steamed	40 min.
cauliflower, flowerets	boiled	8-10 min.
cauliflower, stem down	boiled	20-30 min.
corn, green, tender	boiled	5-10 min.
	steamed	15 min.
	baked	20 min.
corn on the cob	boiled	8-10 min.
	steamed	15 min.
eggplant, whole	boiled	30 min.
	steamed	40 min.
	baked	45 min.
parsnips	boiled	25-40 min.
	steamed	60 min.
	baked	60-75 min.
peas, green	boiled or steamed	5-15 min.
potatoes	boiled	20-40 min.
	steamed	60 min.
	baked	45-60 min.
pumpkin or squash	boiled	20-40 min.
	steamed	45 min.
	baked	60 min.
tomatoes	boiled	5-15 min.
turnips	boiled	25-40 min.

DRYING TIME TABLE

Fruit	Sugar or Honey	Cooking Time
apricots	¼ c. for each cup of fruit	about 40 min.
figs	1 T. for each cup of fruit	about 30 min.
peaches	¼ c. for each cup of fruit	about 45 min.
prunes	2 T. for each cup of fruit	about 45 min.

VEGETABLES & FRUITS

BUYING FRESH VEGETABLES

Artichokes: Look for compact, tightly closed heads with green, clean-looking leaves. Avoid those with leaves that are brown or separated.

Asparagus: Stalks should be tender and firm; tips should be close and compact. Choose the stalks with very little white; they are more tender. Use asparagus soon because it toughens quickly.

Beans, Snap: Those with small seeds inside the pods are best. Avoid beans with dry-looking pods.

Broccoli, Brussels Sprouts and Cauliflower: Flower clusters on broccoli and cauliflower should be tight and close together. Brussels sprouts should be firm and compact. Smudgy, dirty spots may indicate pests or disease.

Cabbage and Head Lettuce: Choose heads that are heavy for their size. Avoid cabbage with worm holes and lettuce with discoloration or soft rot.

Cucumbers: Choose long, slender cucumbers for best quality. May be dark or medium green, but yellow ones are undesirable.

Mushrooms: Caps should be closed around the stems. Avoid black or brown gills.

Peas and Lima Beans: Select pods that are well-filled but not bulging. Avoid dried, spotted, yellow or limp pods.

BUYING FRESH FRUITS

Bananas: Skin should be free of bruises and black or brown spots. Purchase them slightly green and allow them to ripen at room temperature.

Berries: Select plump, solid berries with good color. Avoid stained containers which indicate wet or leaky berries. Berries with clinging caps, such as blackberries and raspberries, may be unripe. Strawberries without caps may be overripe.

Melons: In cantaloupes, thick, close netting on the rind indicates best quality. Cantaloupes are ripe when the stem scar is smooth and the space between the netting is yellow or yellow-green. They are best when fully ripe with fruity odor.

Honeydews are ripe when rind has creamy to yellowish color and velvety texture. Immature honeydews are whitish-green.

Ripe watermelons have some yellow color on one side. If melons are white or pale green on one side, they are not ripe.

Oranges, Grapefruit and Lemons: Choose those heavy for their size. Smoother, thinner skins usually indicate more juice. Most skin markings do not affect quality. Oranges with a slight greenish tinge may be just as ripe as fully colored ones. Light or greenish-yellow lemons are more tart than deep yellow ones. Avoid citrus fruits showing withered, sunken or soft areas.

NAPKIN FOLDING

FOR BEST RESULTS, use well-starched linen napkins if possible. For more complicated folds, 24-inch napkins work best. Practice the folds with newspapers. Children will have fun decorating the table once they learn these attractive folds!

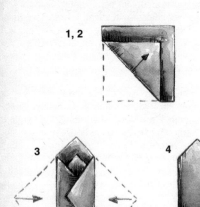

SHIELD

Easy fold. Elegant with monogram in corner.

Instructions:
1. Fold into quarter size. If monogrammed, ornate corner should face down.
2. Turn up folded corner three-quarters.
3. Overlap right side and left side points.
4. Turn over; adjust sides so they are even, single point in center.
5. Place point up or down on plate, or left of plate.

ROSETTE

Elegant on plate.

Instructions:
1. Fold left and right edges to center, leaving ½" opening along center.
2. Pleat firmly from top edge to bottom edge. Sharpen edges with hot iron.
3. Pinch center together. If necessary, use small piece of pipe cleaner to secure and top with single flower.
4. Spread out rosette.

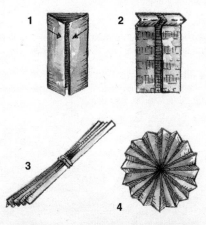

NAPKIN FOLDING

1

2

3

CANDLE

Easy to do; can be decorated.

Instructions:
1. Fold into triangle, point at top.
2. Turn lower edge up 1".
3. Turn over, folded edge down.
4. Roll tightly from left to right.
5. Tuck in corner. Stand upright.

FAN

Pretty in napkin ring or on plate.

Instructions:
1. Fold top and bottom edges to center.
2. Fold top and bottom edges to center a second time.
3. Pleat firmly from the left edge. Sharpen edges with hot iron.
4. Spread out fan. Balance flat folds of each side on table. Well-starched napkins will hold shape.

1, 2

4

3

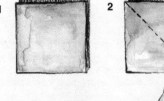

1

2

3, 4

5

LILY

Effective and pretty on table.

Instructions:
1. Fold napkin into quarters.
2. Fold into triangle, closed corner to open points.
3. Turn two points over to other side. (Two points are on either side of closed point.)
4. Pleat.
5. Place closed end in glass. Pull down two points on each side and shape.

MEASUREMENTS & SUBSTITUTIONS

MEASUREMENTS

a pinch	1/8 teaspoon or less
3 teaspoons	1 tablespoon
4 tablespoons	1/4 cup
8 tablespoons	1/2 cup
12 tablespoons	3/4 cup
16 tablespoons	1 cup
2 cups	1 pint
4 cups	1 quart
4 quarts	1 gallon
8 quarts	1 peck
4 pecks	1 bushel
16 ounces	1 pound
32 ounces	1 quart
1 ounce liquid	2 tablespoons
8 ounces liquid	1 cup

Use standard measuring spoons and cups. All measurements are level.

C° TO F° CONVERSION

120° C	250° F
140° C	275° F
150° C	300° F
160° C	325° F
180° C	350° F
190° C	375° F
200° C	400° F
220° C	425° F
230° C	450° F

Temperature conversions are estimates.

SUBSTITUTIONS

Ingredient	Quantity	Substitute
baking powder	1 teaspoon	1/4 tsp. baking soda plus 1/2 tsp. cream of tartar
chocolate	1 square (1 oz.)	3 or 4 T. cocoa plus 1 T. butter
cornstarch	1 tablespoon	2 T. flour or 2 tsp. quick-cooking tapioca
cracker crumbs	3/4 cup	1 c. bread crumbs
dates	1 lb.	1 1/2 c. dates, pitted and cut
dry mustard	1 teaspoon	1 T. prepared mustard
flour, self-rising	1 cup	1 c. all-purpose flour, 1/2 tsp. salt, and 1 tsp. baking powder
herbs, fresh	1 tablespoon	1 tsp. dried herbs
ketchup or chili sauce	1 cup	1 c. tomato sauce plus 1/2 c. sugar and 2 T. vinegar (for use in cooking)
milk, sour	1 cup	1 T. lemon juice or vinegar plus sweet milk to make 1 c. (let stand 5 minutes)
whole	1 cup	1/2 c. evaporated milk plus 1/2 c. water
min. marshmallows	10	1 lg. marshmallow
onion, fresh	1 small	1 T. instant minced onion, rehydrated
sugar, brown	1/2 cup	2 T. molasses in 1/2 c. granulated sugar
powdered	1 cup	1 c. granulated sugar plus 1 tsp. cornstarch
tomato juice	1 cup	1/2 c. tomato sauce plus 1/2 c. water

When substituting cocoa for chocolate in cakes, the amount of flour must be reduced. Brown and white sugars usually can be interchanged.

EQUIVALENCY CHART

Food	Quantity	Yield
apple	1 medium	1 cup
banana, mashed	1 medium	1/3 cup
bread	1 1/2 slices	1 cup soft crumbs
bread	1 slice	1/4 cup fine, dry crumbs
butter	1 stick or 1/4 pound	1/2 cup
cheese, American, cubed	1 pound	2 2/3 cups
American, grated	1 pound	5 cups
cream cheese	3-ounce package	6 2/3 tablespoons
chocolate, bitter	1 square	1 ounce
cocoa	1 pound	4 cups
coconut	1 1/2 pound package	2 2/3 cups
coffee, ground	1 pound	5 cups
cornmeal	1 pound	3 cups
cornstarch	1 pound	3 cups
crackers, graham	14 squares	1 cup fine crumbs
saltine	28 crackers	1 cup fine crumbs
egg	4 - 5 whole	1 cup
whites	8 - 10	1 cup
yolks	10 - 12	1 cup
evaporated milk	1 cup	3 cups whipped
flour, cake, sifted	1 pound	4 1/2 cups
rye	1 pound	5 cups
white, sifted	1 pound	4 cups
white, unsifted	1 pound	3 3/4 cups
gelatin, flavored	3 1/4 ounces	1/2 cup
unflavored	1/4 ounce	1 tablespoon
lemon	1 medium	3 tablespoon juice
marshmallows	16	1/4 pound
noodles, cooked	8-ounce package	7 cups
uncooked	4 ounces (1 1/2 cups)	2 - 3 cups cooked
macaroni, cooked	8-ounce package	6 cups
macaroni, uncooked	4 ounces (1 1/4 cups)	2 1/4 cups cooked
spaghetti, uncooked	7 ounces	4 cups cooked
nuts, chopped	1/4 pound	1 cup
almonds	1 pound	3 1/2 cups
walnuts, broken	1 pound	3 cups
walnuts, unshelled	1 pound	1 1/2 to 1 3/4 cups
onion	1 medium	1/2 cup
orange	3 - 4 medium	1 cup juice
raisins	1 pound	3 1/2 cups
rice, brown	1 cup	4 cups cooked
converted	1 cup	3 1/2 cups cooked
regular	1 cup	3 cups cooked
wild	1 cup	4 cups cooked
sugar, brown	1 pound	2 1/2 cups
powdered	1 pound	3 1/2 cups
white	1 pound	2 cups
vanilla wafers	22	1 cup fine crumbs
zwieback, crumbled	4	1 cup

FOOD QUANTITIES

FOR LARGE SERVINGS

	25 Servings	50 Servings	100 Servings
Beverages:			
coffee	1/2 pound & 1 1/2 gallons water	1 pound & 3 gallons water	2 pounds & 6 gallons water
lemonade	10 - 15 lemons & 1 1/2 gallons water	20 - 30 lemons & 3 gallons water	40 - 60 lemons & 6 gallons water
tea	1/12 pound & 1 1/2 gallons water	1/6 pound & 3 gallons water	1/3 pound & 6 gallons water
Desserts:			
layered cake	1 12" cake	3 10" cakes	6 10" cakes
sheet cake	1 10" x 12" cake	1 12" x 20" cake	2 12" x 20" cakes
watermelon	37 1/2 pounds	75 pounds	150 pounds
whipping cream	3/4 pint	1 1/2 to 2 pints	3 - 4 pints
Ice cream:			
brick	3 1/4 quarts	6 1/2 quarts	13 quarts
bulk	2 1/4 quarts	4 1/2 quarts or 1 1/4 gallons	9 quarts or 2 1/2 gallons
Meat, poultry or fish:			
fish	13 pounds	25 pounds	50 pounds
fish, fillets or steak	7 1/2 pounds	15 pounds	30 pounds
hamburger	9 pounds	18 pounds	35 pounds
turkey or chicken	13 pounds	25 - 35 pounds	50 - 75 pounds
wieners (beef)	6 1/2 pounds	13 pounds	25 pounds
Salads, casseroles:			
baked beans	3/4 gallon	1 1/4 gallons	2 1/2 gallons
jello salad	3/4 gallon	1 1/4 gallons	2 1/2 gallons
potato salad	4 1/4 quarts	2 1/4 gallons	4 1/2 gallons
scalloped potatoes	4 1/2 quarts or 1 12" x 20" pan	9 quarts or 2 1/4 gallons	18 quarts 4 1/2 gallons
spaghetti	1 1/4 gallons	2 1/2 gallons	5 gallons
Sandwiches:			
bread	50 slices or 3 1-lb. loaves	100 slices or 6 1-lb. loaves	200 slices or 12 1-lb. loaves
butter	1/2 pound	1 pound	2 pounds
lettuce	1 1/2 heads	3 heads	6 heads
mayonnaise	1 cup	2 cups	4 cups
mixed filling			
meat, eggs, fish	1 1/2 quarts	3 quarts	6 quarts
jam, jelly	1 quart	2 quarts	4 quarts

COOKING TERMS

Au gratin: Topped with crumbs and/or cheese and browned in oven or under broiler.

Au jus: Served in its own juices.

Baste: To moisten foods during cooking with pan drippings or special sauce in order to add flavor and prevent drying.

Bisque: A thick cream soup.

Blanch: To immerse in rapidly boiling water and allow to cook slightly.

Cream: To soften a fat, especially butter, by beating it at room temperature. Butter and sugar are often creamed together, making a smooth, soft paste.

Crimp: To seal the edges of a two-crust pie either by pinching them at intervals with the fingers or by pressing them together with the tines of a fork.

Crudités: An assortment of raw vegetables (i.e. carrots, broccoli, celery, mushrooms) that is served as an hors d'oeuvre, often accompanied by a dip.

Degrease: To remove fat from the surface of stews, soups or stock. Usually cooled in the refrigerator so that fat hardens and is easily removed.

Dredge: To coat lightly with flour, corn-meal, etc.

Entrée: The main course.

Fold: To incorporate a delicate substance, such as whipped cream or beaten egg whites, into another substance without releasing air bubbles. A spatula is used to gently bring part of the mixture from the bottom of the bowl to the top. The process is repeated, while slowly rotating the bowl, until the ingredients are thoroughly blended.

Glaze: To cover with a glossy coating, such as a melted and somewhat diluted jelly for fruit desserts.

Julienne: To cut or slice vegetables, fruits or cheeses into match-shaped slivers.

Marinate: To allow food to stand in a liquid in order to tenderize or to add flavor.

Meuniére: Dredged with flour and sautéed in butter.

Mince: To chop food into very small pieces.

Parboil: To boil until partially cooked; to blanch. Usually final cooking in a seasoned sauce follows this procedure.

Pare: To remove the outermost skin of a fruit or vegetable.

Poach: To cook gently in hot liquid kept just below the boiling point.

Purée: To mash foods by hand by rubbing through a sieve or food mill, or by whirling in a blender or food processor until per-fectly smooth.

Refresh: To run cold water over food that has been parboiled in order to stop the cooking process quickly.

Sauté: To cook and/or brown food in a small quantity of hot shortening.

Scald: To heat to just below the boiling point, when tiny bubbles appear at the edge of the saucepan.

Simmer: To cook in liquid just below the boiling point. The surface of the liquid should be barely moving, broken from time to time by slowly rising bubbles.

Steep: To let food stand in hot liquid in order to extract or to enhance flavor, like tea in hot water or poached fruit in syrup.

Toss: To combine ingredients with a re-peated lifting motion.

Whip: To beat rapidly in order to incorpo-rate air and produce expansion, as in heavy cream or egg whites.

MICROWAVE
HINTS

PRACTICALLY EVERYONE has experienced that dreadful moment in the kitchen when a recipe failed and dinner guests have arrived. Perhaps a failed timer, distraction or a missing or mismeasured ingredient is to blame. These handy tips can save the day!

Acidic foods – Sometimes a tomato-based sauce will become too acidic. Add baking soda, one teaspoon at a time, to the sauce. Use sugar as a sweeter alternative.

Burnt food on pots and pans – Allow the pan to cool on its own. Remove as much of the food as possible. Fill with hot water and add a capful of liquid fabric softener to the pot; let it stand for a few hours. You'll have an easier time removing the burnt food.

Chocolate seizes – Chocolate can seize (turn coarse and grainy) when it comes into contact with water. Place seized chocolate in a metal bowl over a large saucepan with an inch of simmering water in it. Over medium heat, slowly whisk in warm heavy cream. Use 1/4 cup cream to 4 ounces of chocolate. The chocolate will melt and become smooth.

Forgot to thaw whipped topping – Thaw in microwave for 1 minute on the defrost setting. Stir to blend well. Do not over thaw!

Hands smell like garlic or onion – Rinse hands under cold water while rubbing them with a large stainless steel spoon.

Hard brown sugar – Place in a paper bag and microwave for a few seconds, or place hard chunks in a food processor.

Jell-O too hard – Heat on a low microwave power setting for a very short time.

Lumpy gravy or sauce – Use a blender, food processor or simply strain.

No tomato juice – Mix 1/2 cup ketchup with 1/2 cup water.

Out of honey – Substitute 1 1/4 cups sugar dissolved in 1 cup water.

Overcooked sweet potatoes or carrots – Softened sweet potatoes and carrots make a wonderful soufflé with the addition of eggs and sugar. Consult your favorite cookbook for a good soufflé recipe. Overcooked sweet potatoes can also be used as pie filling.

Sandwich bread is stale – Toast or microwave bread briefly. Otherwise, turn it into bread crumbs. Bread exposed to light and heat will hasten its demise, so consider using a bread box. If the bread will not be eaten within a few days, store half in the freezer.

Soup, sauce, gravy too thin – Add 1 tablespoon of flour to hot soup, sauce or gravy. Whisk well (to avoid lumps) while the mixture is boiling. Repeat if necessary.

Sticky rice – Rinse rice with warm water.

Stew or soup is greasy – Refrigerate and remove grease once it congeals. Another trick is to lay cold lettuce leaves over the hot stew for about 10 seconds and then remove. Repeat as necessary.

Too salty – Add a little sugar and vinegar. For soups or sauces, add a raw peeled potato.

Too sweet – Add a little vinegar or lemon juice.

Undercooked cakes and cookies – Serve over vanilla ice cream. You can also layer pieces of cake or cookies with whipped cream and fresh fruit to form a dessert parfait. Crumbled cookies also make an excellent ice cream or cream pie topping.

MICROWAVE HINTS

- Soften hard ice cream by microwaving at 30% power. One pint will take 15–30 seconds; one quart takes 30–45 seconds; one-half gallon takes 45–60 seconds.

- One stick of butter or margarine will soften in 40 seconds when microwaved at 50% power.

- Soften one unwrapped 8-ounce package of cream cheese by placing in a glass bowl and microwaving on high for 15 seconds.

- A carton of whipped topping will thaw in 1 minute on the defrost setting. Whipped topping should be slightly firm in the center, but will blend when stirred. Do not over thaw!

- To scald milk, cook 1 cup for 2–2 1/2 minutes, stirring once each minute.

- Melt half of a 7-ounce jar of marshmallow creme by microwaving on high for 35–40 seconds.

- If Jell-O® has set up too hard, heat on low power for a very short time.

- To soften hardened brown sugar, place package in the microwave and heat for 30 seconds; fluff with a fork and use immediately.

- Warm pancake syrup by heating on high in serving container for 30–60 seconds.

- To restore crystallized honey, heat in a glass jar covered with plastic wrap on high for 30–45 seconds. Repeat if necessary.

- To toast coconut, spread 1/2 cup coconut on a plate and cook for 3–4 minutes; stirring every 30 seconds after 2 minutes. Keep a close watch because it quickly browns.

- To melt chocolate, place 1/2 pound in a glass bowl or measuring cup. Melt uncovered at 50% power for 1–2 minutes; remove and stir. Repeat in 30 second intervals, as needed.

- Plump dried fruits by microwaving 1 cup of water for 1–2 minutes or until boiling. Add 1/2 cup dried fruit and let stand for 5–10 minutes.

- To get more juice out of lemons, microwave on high for 10–20 seconds. Roll on the counter, slice, and juice.

- Crisp stale potato chips, crackers, cookies, or cereal by placing on paper towels and heating in the microwave for 20–30 seconds.

- To make dry bread crumbs, cut 6 slices of bread into 1/2 inch cubes. Microwave in 3-quart casserole for 6–7 minutes or until dry; stir after 3 minutes. Crush in blender.

- To clean your microwave, heat a glass bowl of water with a small amount of vinegar for 5 minutes. Keep the door closed for 5 more minutes to give the steam time to work. Remove the bowl and use a moist, soapy dish cloth to wipe the inside walls and door of your microwave. Dried food should wipe off easily.

MORRIS PRESS COOKBOOKS

Publish Your Own
COOKBOOK

Churches, schools, organizations, families, and businesses can preserve their favorite recipes by publishing a custom cookbook. Cookbooks make a great **fundraiser** because they are easy to sell and highly profitable. Our low prices also make cookbooks a perfect, affordable **keepsake**. We offer:

- Low prices, high quality, and prompt service.
- Many options and styles to suit your needs.
- An online cookbook builder or we can assist.
- 90 days to pay and a written No-Risk Guarantee.

Request a FREE Cookbook Kit to start

Visit **www.morriscookbooks.com/CB**

or call **800-445-6621, ext. CB**

All the Ingredients
for Success!®